It's About Time

It's About Time

Poems

Stanley Moss

HOPEWELL PRESS

Acknowledgments:

American Poetry Review, The New Yorker, PN Review, Times Literary Supplement, The New Republic, Poem, Poetry, Poetry Daily, Poetry London, Virginia Quarterly Review, The Los Angeles Times, The East Hampton Star, The Drunken Boat, New Letters, The London Magazine.

Much thanks to Carcanet Press in the UK for assigning poems from *No Tear Is Commonplace* (2013)

Cover Design by S.M.
Cover Art: Detail from *Salvataggio Miracoloso* by Girolamo Forabosco
Typeset by Hopewell Press
Distributed by The University Press of New England

Library of Congress Cataloging-in-Publication Data

Moss, Stanley.
[Poems. Selections]
It's about time : poems / Stanley Moss.
pages ; cm
ISBN 978-1-937679-55-2 (alk. paper)
I. Title.
PS3563.O885A6 2015
811'.54--dc23

2015012622

All inquiries and permission requests should be addressed to the publisher:

Hopewell Press
PO Box 633
Red Hook, NY 12571

Dieu est le seul être qui, pour régner,
n'ait même pas besoin d'exister.

Charles Baudelaire

Whatever their personal faith,
all poets, as such,
are polytheists.

W.H. Auden

The wilderness and the solitary place shall be glad for them;
and the desert shall rejoice, and blossom as the rose.

Isaiah 35:1

To departed friends: human, canine, arboreal, avian

CONTENTS

Sunrise—Morning

12 Noon

Sunset—Night

Eclipse

Merry-Go-Round
Early Poems

Sunrise—Morning

The Poem of Self

I often write in my diary the obsolete poem of self
with my obsolescent pen and ink.
So I throw a poem for a lark, like my hat,
off the Brooklyn Bridge, where Hart Crane, bless him,
"dumped the ashes of his dad in a condom,"
I was told.
I watch my hat glide toward the Atlantic,
wait for a miraculous rescue—
but my poem-hat alights, drifts, sinks down
among the bottom feeders,
the fluke, crab, catfish in sewage
of the East River, still musical, distantly related
to the North Sea. I hope my drowned hat
shelters blind, half-dead newborns
that lip the taste of my sweatband,
the taste of me their first breakfast
of undigested unleavened waste.
The River Styx has clean water where Elijah
swims with the Angels Gabriel and Raphael.

So the poem of self gone,
poetry must face, may two-face,
must honor the language, point out to readers
the garden of delights, hell to paradise,
almost, but never seen before.
Are the playhouses of God metaphors?
Is God rhyme? The God of everyone obsolete?
Then in the beginning was the Word,
the Word, let's say, Fish, a live-bearer—

the fish grew fins, then feet,
asked questions without answers.
To wish or not to wish that is the question.
Every word is a question.
Put a question mark after each word,
the question mark is a fish breaking water:
poetry? mother? anything? kiss? glory?
So remembering and forgetting are over,
useless boredom is plagiarized,
human beings are spawned,
trees genuflect, there are
Stop! Look! and Listen! prayers
at railroad crossings.
Truth is, *je, yo, ich,*
a Former Obsolete First-Person Pronoun,
stole the word "so" from a friend—
seems a petty theft but is a felony
when the word packs a deadly weapon.

Looking back, God is a verb, adjective,
article, contraction, infinitive, any part of speech,
any language, since every living thing speaks God.
God is a verb—
"He was godded once by the Lord,"
means created or killed, and God is a noun,
adjective, article, infinitive, any part of speech,
birdsong, neigh, hee-haw,
bark, bray, buzz, all God's speech.

Now the poem of *you* is obsolete
and the poem of *he, she, we* obsolete—penis and vagina,
mouth, anus, hands
holding on for dear life to each other,
everything that dreams obsolete,
everything but what in the good old days we called "love."
Now Johann Sebastian Bach
is a verb. Bach you! Bach you!
So help us or don't help us, God,
we have the luxury of tears, others weep
with fluttering wings, falling leaves, so help us
or don't help us, God,
breaking my vow, so help me God.

July 4

Thank you for the clover that bloomed today
full of bees after last night's rain. July 4th
seems just as it was under the British,
the day Jefferson, age 33, and the Fathers
signed the Declaration they wrote together,
not the rough draft
that demanded the right to close slave markets
but the soiled version I fly the flag for.
The same apple and pear trees are here.
There is a Continental Congress of birds,
seeds of equality planted by the winds,
insects and fallen fruit,
things living with and without hearts.
Some animals, bless them, are free
despite dry walls, hunters' guns and traps,
everyone a creature of the times, like us,
a few, like John Adams, farmed without slaves.
I read glacial writing, the Hudson river
demanding on granite cliffs
freedom of speech, religion, and assembly.

Often, private property was not theft,
but murder: there were promissory notes
and paper money that "bought and sold Men."
Some died in the earthquake of slavery,
some in today's after tremors,
some were burned alive, crippled, turned to stone
by the filthy-mouthed volcanoes of hate.
On the 4th of July I celebrate the preamble,

the runaways, the everyday decent folks
who do not need revenge, and those who did.

I remember: via the Spanish ambassador
the Infante in '75 sent Benjamin Franklin
his translation of Sallust's *Historiae.*
Franklin sent back by packet boat his views
"the Muses have scarcely visited these remote regions"
so he provided the Continental Congress'
Declaration of Causes and Necessity of Taking Up Arms.
Washington's army was soon to escape from Brooklyn
across New York harbor because the wind
was right and there was fog. My darling Deist thought
rebellion against tyrants is obedience to God.

Parable of the Porcupine

The only animal that cries real tears,
my porcupine weeps in terror of Sancho, my good dog.
A crown of thorns crawls under the lilacs.
With her just-born swaddled in quills,
nursing her child, impossible piglet,
she scrawls in mud, in rodent Aramaic,
something like, "Do not touch me."
Touched by two mouths now and first needles,
bless you for hiding in your sepulcher of leaves
while Sancho, his mouth full of quills,
in faith and hope rests his painful head in my lap.

Bright Day

Vivo sin vivir en mí,
y de tal manera espero,
que muero porque no muero.
              —*Santa Theresa de Ávila*

I call out this morning: Hello, hello.
I proclaim the bright day of the soul.
The sun is a good fellow
the Devil's my kind of guy. No deaths today I know.
I live because I live. I do not die
because I do not die.
In Tuscan sunlight Masaccio
painted his belief that St. Peter's shadow
cured a cripple, gave him back his sight.
My shadow is a useless asshole, a nether eyebrow.
I walk in morning sunlight,
where trees demonstrate against death.
There's danger, when I die my soul may rise in wrath.
I know the dark night of the soul
does not need God's Eye
as a beggar does not need a hand or a bowl.
In my garden, death questions every root, flowers reply.

Parable of the Book-Man

Half man, half book, he spent the day
reading himself, the night
half in bed, half on the shelf.
He did not like to turn his own pages
so he went to sea, slept in a hammock. The Northwind
abducting Orithyia turned his pages.
The Atlantic turned him forward, backward, forward.

In a deserted forest, above the beach, a sailor
on shore leave, he sat on an oak stump,
watched a heartless fire ant
peacefully working her way down the bark.
Frightened by the book-man
she let off a God-given scent that warned
slender-waisted subjects
slowly moving a mountain down to an anthill:
Danger! Never surrender!
Their civilization, almost all female,
prospered. Even so, sisters and half sisters
battled other nations, red carpenter ants,
the dead uncountable,
while queens and gallants were safe in bed
or sipping nectar in a gorgeous peony.
Despite so many reasons to be dead,
how many reasons were there to be alive?
Book-man on the beach, his kind outlasted
by continents of ants.
The littles will outlive all tears and laughter—
nothing left with a dangerous heart.

Still, it is and was better to be human
while God plays a game of horseshoes,
throws wreaths of life and death
around our necks, some saintly leaners.

Pax Poetica

The earth needs peace more than it needs the moon,
that beauty without which the oceans lose their intellect.
Peace in bombed gardens where butterflies swoon
into the sun, living one day and dying in the shelling
of that night, where joyous rat and knife inspect
the numerous wares the dead are selling.
The earth needs peace more than it needs the moon.
Sometimes the dead lie hand in hand: six, seven, eight
after a night of minuses and endless decrease,
they do not serve, or stand or wait,
they unpeople themselves flogged in the sun.
No caesura. No rainbow. No peace.
I pity the poets who think that war will be undone
by poetry, the hate-filled world saved by music. I am one. . .
A little more time and poetry will set things straight.
It took time to find the Golden Fleece.
The useless dead hang in markets of the sun,
alone as pork thighs. Every morning comes and goes
more quickly. I know where wild thyme blows,
that naked beauty steals naked to my arms, then goes
to pay a debt to sorrow. No peace.
In a sometime-sometime land, there will be no joy in killing.
We are meant to hold each other but not for keeping;
we kill—just as the toad cannot keep from leaping.
In the grave there is no work or device
nor knowledge nor wisdom, I read in *Ecclesiastes.*
Still, fishermen lift their nets, hoist death weeping,
throw back death twinkling like a small coin into the profitless seas.
Look, the eternal fish swims away leaping.
Moonless, we still have starlight, the aurora borealis,
fires above the Conqueror Worm and beneath
till the sun runs off with the earth in its teeth.

Paper Swallow

Francisco Goya y Lucientes,
I dedicate this paper swallow to you and fly it
from the balcony of San Antonio de la Florida
past the empty chapels of the four doctors of the church.
My praying hands are fish fins again,
one eye a lump of tar, the other hard blood,
my flapping lids sewed down to my cheekbones.
Time, the invisible snake, keeps its head
and fangs deep in the vagina of space.
Reason blinded me, banished me.
I fight the liar in me, selective desire,
my calling nightmares "dreamless sleep."
Blind, *coño*, I made a musical watch,
the image of Don Quixote points the hours,
Sancho the minute hand. I hear the right time
when I listen to my watch play church bells.
Mystery this, mystery that.
I have another watch—wolves howling and dogs barking.
Now the invisible snake swims in the Ebro.
I look out of my window to see time
as if it were not in my mouth
and all my other two-timing orifices.
Don Francisco, I swear at the feet of the dead who maim me
and the living who heal me that the least sound,
a page turning, whips me. I owe my blindness,
this paper swallow, to you, because I lived
most of my life, a *marrano*, in your deaf house.
I pull open one of my eyes like the jaws of a beast.

Fantasy on a Goya Drawing

Father Goya told me
after the puppets were cut to pieces
you, Franciscan or Jew,
began the year in an ungodly place,
your head collared, protruding
from dead Rocinante's asshole,
the horse's belly lanced open
then laced with cord like a boot.
A commoner, you wrestled
through the stench, through the offal and bowels—
barking dogs around your gray head.

A week before, you did not celebrate
Christ's birthday as your own, as a Russian poet did.
You did not finish your book of unhappy deaths
as Cervantes finished his sacred, funny book,
the master, five years an Algerian slave,
his left arm sacrificed at Lepanto.

Mi papá Goya told me, under the arch
of a bridge not traveled, it was you
who killed the knight's horse
and crawled in, worked your head out
of a stained-ass window. You died living,
these your last words:
I've seen my face and a cloud reflected in a well
but only the sun and moon reflect in a puddle of blood.

En Zaragoza à mediados del siglo pasado, me
tieron à un alguacil llamado Lampiños, en el cuer
no de un Rocin muerto, y lo cosieron; toda la noche

Song of Barbed Wire

I've heard the red deer of Eastern Europe
climb with their fawns up rocky hills
to graze on poor patches of grass
rather than go down to green valleys
that once were cut off by barbed wire,
'round national borders and death camps.
They respect, fear, remember
the razor wire no longer there.

I graze on fables:
thou-shalt-nots passed on by deer-talk,
that has the sound of our long wet kisses—
buck to doe to fawn, nose to nose. I hear
commandments sent by antlers scraping trees,
received like the color of eyes.

Nazi and Stalinist barbed wire words
send me up a hill to graze.
I know my red deer-like progenitors
passed on to me a need to suck,
to be afraid of fire.
When I try to kiss my way into green valleys
I am afraid to move beyond the human,
I am not naked, wrapped in barbed razor wire.
There is an original blessing.

Poem

Teacher of reading, of "you will not" and "you shall,"
almighty Grammarian author of Genesis,
whether language holds three forms of the future
as Hebrew does or no future tense at all
like Chinese, may it perform a public service,
offer the protection of the Great Wall,
the hope and sorrow of the Western Wall.

Death Is a Dream

Death is a dream. Time,
perhaps the illegitimate sister of silence,
mother of space, is seldom dealt with
as a living thing, male or female,
male and female. Time "worships language,"
does not kneel but is a passionate lover
with respect and disrespect
for what is or ever was.
Again, time lives! "Again" is a word
that tries to cage time in
as does the phrase "ever was,"
but the cage is just a grammatical mirror,
without a right or wrong

I have a lover's quarrel with the followers
of life is a dream. Time
sits at table with a musical family,
sitting and reading from left to right:
free verse, iamb, spondee, Alexandrian, trimeter,
inflected and uninflected languages,
dear cousins, ancient aunts and uncles.

In a dark, repertory theater death is a dream.
Time stands in the pit. She is also an actor.
Like the universe, the theater is empty and a full house.
The play's "The End of Everything," a light-year's farce.
The action: Rights and Wrongs, each plays the other,
changes costume on stage. Then speechless tragedy:
time measures space inch by inch—

the pity is, in the end she turns back,
unmeasures herself and every other thing.
Death is a dream without measure, no light-years,
no days, no meters, no milestones,
no paces, no walls or fences,
no pints or half-pints, no pounds, no ounces,
no cubits, no handbreadths.

*

Mozart's music prolongs my life,
but his *Requiem* could not prolong his.
I stand on a soapbox in Washington Square,
flying the stars and stripes.
I speak to dog-walkers, the homeless,
any passerby:
if death is a dream, it is something else,
without a face, without heaven or hell.
Death is not eternal, will dream and die.
The question is, just before death dies
is there a kind of waking up,
a slapstick *Liebestod*?
Summer dresses as winter,
night and day fall in love,
die in each others arms.
I am proud time lets me stand here, sit at table
from time to time, so to speak, with the family.
We are communal, like the Jews at the Last Supper.
I had a dream I saw a giant silver sea bass
swimming in sky as if it were ocean.

56,000-Year Poem

This morning I'm part me, part anything.
In my notebook I uselessly draw
a leaf, a rat that loves a cat, Fatima's hand.
After anywhere, any place, secondhand,
I set down words on blue lines, like pigeons
flying through the open doors of the British Museum,
or crows on a fence.
I remember . . . a Renaissance painting,
three astrologers, I believe the Magi,
at rest in the desert their faces look inward,
sextant, hour glass, charts beside them—
the intelligence of clouds in the morning sky.
They cross the painted desert without words.
Beyond the reach of their prayers,
they find a Child stabled with His mother,
linger . . . witness the circumcision,
then journey homeward in the dead of winter.
I gnaw a bone of Spanish poetry.
A thousand years of illumination and wars,
the cow becomes a symbol of Christianity,
the donkey is the Jews. In my España,
protected by Maria and Guardia Civil,
at Easter they slaughter a donkey to please the Child.
Reader, come a little closer, have a whiskey.
Before the stars were named, before there was prayer,
some 55,000 years ago when there were
perhaps 10,000 worldly Homo sapiens,
the DNA in my spit shows
my ancestors hunted in what is now Iberia.

Darling, hairy great-grandfather
to the hundredth power, I blow you a kiss.
I point to your nose and my nose and smile.
I point to the sun and say, *the sun, el sol.*
I point to the moon and say, *the moon, la luna.*
A democrat, I look the other way.
I see a thousand years of grandchildren.
My skull blows them a kiss. Margaret
kisses back (I hope my mother's name is still useful).
I hope she's heard of Hamlet, speaks some English.
I say to my distant granddaughter, *Jew,*
tell me what you know about the stars.
A penny for your thoughts.

Seems

It doesn't take one day for water
to turn into three feet of ice.
                    – Chinese Proverb

Changing right to wrong takes time
or never happens. Changing wrong to right
takes longer or never happens. Life to death,
death to life is no walk in the countryside.
Under three feet of ice, an old brook flows
into an ice and snow silenced river
that empties into the understanding ocean.
Who can say, "Seems, seems, I know not seems"—
words never spoken by the Prince of Peace?
All water has a face. Oceans welcome,
do not devour rivers and brooks.
In winter, rivers and brooks
become oceans' beards and eyebrows.
Old to young happens—an old North wind
becomes a summer breeze.

A Misfortune

To idle without direction is best,
forget north, east, south and west.
It's up and down, out and in,
no room at the inn, and, and
I love a Bernini fountain.
My mother still takes my hand,
leads me in and out of my mind.
My footprints are all I leave behind
any time of the night or day
waves may wash them away.
The truth: it's better to be a whale
than a snail,
better to be a bard
than a postcard,
I'd rather be this than that,
I'd rather be a shoe than a hat,
I'll take a chance
that sometime I'll dance,
Lord, sitting on the fence
is better than pretense
but there's a lot to be said for nonsense.

Two Arias

In an empty house I'm trying to sing a high F,
you've heard my baritone and bass,
tonight I'm coloratura, I'm the Queen of the Night,
from a mountaintop I reach out my arms,
open my wings, lift a clawed foot and sing:
"O do not tremble, my dear son,
it is the penis and vagina that hear confession,
nipples are saints, the orgasm gives absolution."

Moonlight is not beyond my authority.
Still, there is a king who mounts my darkness
with lion head and eagle-claw feet—my nation.
After, later,
a certain sadness in my haunches I call dawn,
I return to my night owls, my nest of dry grass and time.
There, there. Everything comes home.

*

Morning, I'm a Hudson Valley baritone.
I live a mile from where, age three, I saw
my first field of wild flowers. I swooned
while my father fixed a flat tire.
Yesterday, twenty-first of June,
I drove through the woods to a concert hall,
road-side wild flowers tuned up, improvised.
I half-forgot music did not come out of
a phonograph, musicians have faces . . .
In good time, the wind blows from all directions.
I tried to live in a house with beauty
constant as gravity.

I tell myself,
you're living in a child's treehouse.
I caught myself saying if I die, rather than when.
I pretended death was a supernumerary,
so I found myself weeping over little things
after I saw friends I love had little strokes.
I watched them grow thin
with occasional trouble speaking—
the thinking *prima ballerina*
has trouble going up and down the stairs.

*

Enough! There's something between gravel and semen,
between seamen and seeing men. Fantastical
sons and daughters, now that I've confused you—
I remind you, when they boiled a kid in its mother's milk,
a tribe said, "Stop!" and "Stop!" when they killed the firstborn.
In time of war, all four-year-olds ask,
"Why do they want to kill me?"
I did not tell you I fell down
ancient cobblestone steps in Jerusalem,
broke my wrist that quickly turned blue,
I wandered the streets and found cool waters,
the well of Lady Miriam (Mary) . . .
Pope John Paul flew overhead in a helicopter.
I was simply trying to make a name for myself,
following the ancient, popular belief
that each person is represented by a star
which appears at birth. Firmament of parliamentarians,
I simply want to be worthy of such an honor
when I sing, buried alone in my tomb,
man in two persons, son and holy ghost.

Revenge Comedy

Running out of time,
I can keep time with my foot,
with or without a shoe.
Truth is, time keeps me.
When I was seven, my mother gave me
a Mickey Mouse watch I hated.
I purposely overwound it.

China has one time zone.
When it is 5 am in Shanghai
and the sun is rising, it is 5 am in West China,
where it is the middle of the night.
My time differs from street to street,
from one side of the room to the other.

So much happened that is always.
So much never happened that is always,
centuries when truth was painted
as the daughter of time.
Hard to believe God pays attention
to what time it is anywhere.
Running out of time,
years, degrees, minutes are dirty little words.

When I was a child I slept as a child,
the sun used to wake me and my mother.
We had intimate conversations while my father slept.
He awoke and lived with nightmares in his eyes,
perplexed, enlightened, without a Guide—

son and assassin, a boy, I was his disciple.
He and I fished with copper line, a gut leader
and a spoon for landlocked salmon.
He caught one beauty. It was, he said,
the happiest moment of his life.
My father was whipped by time
and he whipped back. I was in the middle.
What was knifing him, cutting out the flesh
under his shell I never understood.

Now I wake at dawn, the sun mothers me.
My father sees to it and I say *okay*,
every day is a school day.
Until I was 50, I never wore a watch,
then like Antonio Machado, I set my watch back
24 hours. My sundial never tells lies
when the sun is down.

Burial of the Gravedigger's Daughter

I'll take her to the hill
Near the olive tree.
Can I do it in the daylight?
I'm afraid what I shall see.

Not all the graves I've dug,
Dry and wide and deep,
Can hold the sweetness
Of my daughter not asleep.

In our village someone
Must dig the graves for all,
Her death has just begun
Under her prayer shawl.

My shovel is my cross.
My shovel cannot bless.
My child, I must soil
Your white lace dress.

What

My first dream came with a gift of *What?*
the infant's first wordless question.
I stand before you a sleepwalker
rubbing out, out the damned spots of yesteryear.
A saint or Zadig invented the words:
"¿qué causa?" "what?" so we might ask honest questions.
In a dream of curiosity, I ask—what,
how, who, which, where, why?
The dream of curiosity stages matters out of the question:
dramas about the living and the dead,
where each often plays the other. A little rouge,
a little powder, a change of wigs, who knows what's what?
Night changes to day, and day to night.
You think it's all sun and moon, not trickery?
True I hold the portfolio *chargé d'affaires* of my life,
but I am a corrupt official, easily bribed
by a tree into saying "beauty is the answer."
I sell visas to Anchorwhat and Paradise.

*

What is an atheist on the temple mount, and way of the cross.
What says "Rome's Wolf is younger than Manhattan's Mastodon."
Rivers of what, what, what, what,
run into the ocean, flood two thirds of the world,
"The poet is the instrument of language,
not the other way around."
Flocks of where, how, which, who, why—fill the sky,
while over Latin American jungles voiceless *Stringbirds*
sound cello-like purple-feathered love calls with their wings—
now stringed instruments—a dark paradoxical gift,
like John Milton's gift of inner sight after his loss of outer sight.

There is no proof that reality simply is what is.
What—does not enter the past but is entered by it.
What—protects the truth by offering itself
as prey to the raptor fact.
The *Stringbird* is never caged,
as gods are caged in houses of worship.
Sometimes I hear its wings calling in the woods.
What . . . happens . . . is never quite comprehended.
What is a tree whose roots are a bear's heart;
the blood of *What* flows in mountain streams and rivers,
past spines of ocean life.
Because Proverbs says,
"The leech has two daughters—
Give and Give! . . . and the fire never says enough"—
I remember Kunitz put in a garden for Cal Lowell
and Caroline, in Ireland. When Stanley returned
in June, he found only wildflowers in rubble.
Still, walking with them across their hillside,
hell and love glances in their eyes,
there was reason to hope because of love,
laughter and nightingales, the lovers might find
the golden bough that once allowed a Roman
to pass safely through the underworld—
but dreadful, unwanted guests were coming.
What's to do? Turn the key, it may unlock or lock the door.

*

Now death is in fashion but life's not out of style,
whatever the hemline, glove or cuff.
I don't see proof death's worthwhile.

It never says *enough*.
I spit in death's ocean.
Death is time away
from here, from everywhere,
today is here,
anterior.
Life and death are hand and glove:
life's the hand, death's the glove.
What caresses my face with love
smacks it with an empty glove,
heavy as the ocean.

Why

I know my love of "whys?" is a faithless sin.
I am a worm. You, Lord, are my Robin.
I think the Holy Spirit is a Crow, a Dove, any bird.
Born beyond redemption, I will never repent,
I curl around the serpent,
temptation to temptation, disobedient.
I never swallowed that You made the firmament, Your Word
that in the beginning was the Word.
I swallow my foolish questions—many "whys?"
I pick from between my teeth the letter "y."
I am not wise. Now I am absurd.

Since there is no place in heaven for curiosity
or anyone with my beliefs,
I will take in the long haul earthly simplicity—
I will sleep with Mother Nature, my weak spot,
perhaps dreaming of questions, not in a Greek pot
but in the dirt among the leaves
parked under an apple tree to rot
in a place less pagan than hallowed ground,
never again to fool around in the company
of any living thing that fools around with me.

One day when I am far from useless,
You will throw me still wriggling in the river of loneliness
while You listen to the praise of gulls, frogs' applause.
"Why? Why? Why?" Your grand answer: "Because."
Old Fool, I have no desire for the afterlife.
I want to stay here with You, to hang around
with Your trees, Your animals and my wife.

12 Noon

Pollen

Still, near Santa Maria in Trastevere,
I saw a painting called *No War* and another, *I Love You,*
by an American woman eating a peach.
I was reborn in old Rome, still remain,
not a marble fragment, not a painting, more like
the Cloaca Maxima, an old, stinking survivor.
Much I had seen I did not recall:
ugliness and beauty, part of me
as music, unfinished work,
the wrong note effect,
—what I wanted to forget
and what I wished to remember,
that her lips upon my flesh
said, "You are changing,"
then, "You will never change."

*

It is time to uncover the mirrors—
there is no death in the family now.
It is time we wear each other's skin,
fur, scales, feathers, our mouths covered with pollen;
let's sing insect and reptilian songs.
It is time for the carnival of love.
I describe *caprichos*, I narrate beauty I fight for—
its protagonists and antagonists battle within the poem
down in the dirt. Beauty has a tale to tell:
ugliness and terror cut out of skin
and marble—a labor Phidias knew something about.

*

I can hear the earthworm's laughter.
Taught to respond to light, cut in half,
each new half responds to light—small stars.
It is time for asterisks, stars that point to human life.
May my liver, kidney and heart severed
recall good times—I was there
and I refuse to get out of here.
My head, severed from my body,
remembers love, perhaps irregular verbs.

*

What happened to pollen? We die without insects and birds.
My friend going blind thinks life is a dream.
I do not know why yet I live to say
I've gone to seed, I'm not sure of my name.
Winds carry pollen to quarreling cornfields,
on the same bush, a rose quarrels with a rose.
This dust produces that mud. I write in mud
with a stick, with my finger or my tooth.
I have found gardeners on their knees,
farm workers bent in the meat-eating sun
no less reverent than nuns. Every man's soul
is an immigrant, enters a new country
without speaking the language, works long hours,
attends night school. Reaching Paradise,
sometimes he longs for the old country, his body.

*

In my ward of ninety-some "casuals"
at St. Albans Naval Hospital
I wrote a love letter for a one-legged marine,
his good leg eaten by rats when he was in the sand under a Jeep.

His last name was Love. On his own,
he dictated the titles of popular songs.
A couple of days later, remaking his bed,
a nurse told me Love died, "surgical shock."
I was entangled, beaten by missing body parts.
Something of my body stays at sea, dismembered.

*

Virgil thought purple was the color of the soul.
Saint Jerome woke from a dream black and blue,
whipped at the judgment seat for reading Latin poets.
My body, bruised, turns purple, is hardly proof
my soul is at home in my body.
I walk knee-deep in a swamp, stinking of heaven.
A two-year-old child says, "How disgusting!"
I am surprised the child knows the word.
Entangled in water lilies and devil's paintbrush,
I'm up to my knees in spirit.
Yes, yes, it pleases me to go into the dark.
These words are body. I try to find something
man made in the sun that is all over the place.

*

It's no time to die, almost everything's left undone.
Angel of Death, fly off with your black wings
with the first flock of starlings,
out of place among swans with your thick, dirty neck!
I am what others abandoned
that I save. Rather than bury my old Bible,
I leave fragile pages to songbirds
that build, warm their nests and eggs with psalms.

Chrysalis

I wonder how my life might twine and untwine
if, like the brontosaurus, I had a second brain
to work my tail from the base of my spine.
Two egos at odds in one bed, two ids
might cause two dreams at once, hybrids,
one sweet, one nightmare: my bottom half in the mouth
of a brontosaurus, long as a railroad train.
She and I do what most would find uncouth.
Same time, I am in bed, young me with a beauty,
dreaming I'm having a birthday party—
I'm spinning, a butterfly breaks free
out of my ear that is a chrysalis,
circles the room, finds an open window, flies south
to join the millions it needs for company.
I wake, it's morning, I read, a good guess,
what I never knew I thought before: poetry—
poets who simply honor the language.
I'm a psalmist with a Miss-directed penis.
Cupid plays at cards with me for kisses.
Venus, who never spanks, spanks me,
whispers to Mars in bed, "It's time you turned the page
on Stanley being Stanley.
I thought he went out of style in the Ice Age."

Winter

Lunatic solatic,
Mrs., Ms., Mr., Master, Misreader
I sign my name ice-skating
on a frozen pond. I skate
a letter "M," circle an "O,"
gracefully skate "S" twice.
Still when spring comes
my name will be unspelled by the sun,
ripple somewhere, water again, cloudy,
water my houseplants.
I would never skate David,
my middle Psalmist name.

Letter to a Poet

1.

We never made love, but still I believe
we share some intimate knowledge,
something no one else in the world knows—
who were your next door neighbors
when you were a child and teenager,
my parents' friends.
We drove to the Chicago World's Fair
that celebrated "A Century of Progress."
(I sang on experimental television
before television, before you were born.)
I remember the sound of their voices,
Hannah's intimate laundry, her wonderful brassiere
hanging in the bathroom—
I smelled the unimaginable.
I remember decent people, that Max bought
78 turns per minute, "classical"
RCA records every week,
a painting showing a Russian maid scrubbing a cello
hung in his music room,
that Hannah gave me tomato juice,
an extraordinary kindness,
instead of half a grapefruit I hated.
Our remembering might help them out of purgatory
if Dante was right. It helps me out. How about you?

2.

Writing this letter, I was slapped in the face
by a mandrake root.

It slipped my mind
how often you came closer to the truth
by making your reader believe what never happened.
Sometimes, lonely, or never lonely, Fernando Pessoa
accomplished this with five different names.

So your brother was born aged 8 or 10
in the intimacy of your bedroom,
you played, talked and bathed together,
your mother soaped you front and back
in an iron, lion-footed tub.
In those days, the soap was *Ivory*,
99% pure.

I will kidnap your brother,
use him as a sister, so he can help
with a poem about Lilly I can never write.
Still, your brother almost got you killed crossing the street.
You simply had to Stop, Look, and Listen to him first.
He did not cross at corners,
but he read lines to you before you wrote them.
For all I know, your neighbors had lilacs
and wild iris in their garden in Woodmere
that was farther away from the Atlantic than it is now,
but still, you could smell the salt in the air
when the fog came in.

Sister Poem

My sister was a Unitarian,
she loved life, the God-given gift of the world.
She did not need Paradise to make her a Christian,
thought all religions that promised Paradise
offered a business relationship with a jealous God.
She made a funny face at the mention of early martyrs
who preferred to be fresh meat for lions
to living in the world, likely as slaves,
rather than praying for show to the Gods
Trajan or Emperor Augustus.
Her Lord preferred His followers deny Him
rather than sacrifice their lives,
He wanted the living to live, love strangers,
their neighbors, the Beatitudes.
She certainly thought it wise to hide your Judaism
from the public fires of the Inquisition;
she damned the excommunicators of Spinoza,
believed in doing what you could honorably do
to stay out of cattle cars.

When I was a small child
I thought my sister Lilly
was mysteriously related to waterlilies,
daylilies, lilies of the valley.
Imitating her handwriting, I made my first *e* and *l.*
I am ashamed, when I was seven, she was four years older,
I wrestled her to the ground to show I was stronger,
proof the state is stronger than language.
Our dog took her side, barked "get off her."

It was a rare day I did not ask, "Lilly read me a story."
When I stood one foot three inches taller,
she gave me her violin. When all I could play was "Long, Long Ago,"
she taught me Mozart and Bach,
that all things in the universe showed the hand of God.

Years passed. I thought prosody survives history.
She read Rimbaud to me in French and English,
and Lorca, whose photo I hung next to my bed.
My sister wrote to me, "please speak at my funeral."
Not long after, I said, "To death there is no consolation…."
I read most of the lines I just wrote.
I insisted the chapel doors and windows were open
to a congregation of birds and insects. Loners
swooped in and out from noon to sunset.
Not a drop of excrement on the mosaic floor.
A hawk dropped a live mouse that prayed to live
on her coffin. She would have liked that.

Coda

My sister Lillian was a Unitarian.
She insisted I not speak at her funeral.
She made necklaces, pressed butterflies.
Her husband invented our famous intercontinental
space rockets, miniaturized atom bombs
so they could be used as tactical weapons.
Her closest friend, who married a Haitian, and Black Americans
were not allowed in his house. She did not protest,
hold her breath, turn blue and faint,
as she did as a child to get what she wanted.
Lillian taught poetry, had four great grandchildren,
she wanted our mother to have a Unitarian funeral.
Our mother was not a Unitarian.
My sister mailed me my mother's ashes
first class. Later, I collected my dad's, buried both
side-by-side, Montauk daisies between—
their unmarked rocks not too close.

For a wedding present two years after our wedding,
my sister gave us a folded check, $25 to "buy a tree"
and a rope ladder to keep on the top floor
in case our house caught fire.
I am grateful to the poet who taught me
how to get closer to something like the truth,
that is my understanding,
an unenumerated right, protected
by the 9th amendment to the Constitution.

A Refreshment

In our new society, all the old religious orders and titles
are ice creams: Rabbis, Priests, Mullahs,
Gurus, Buddhists, Shiites, Sunni, Dominicans,
Franciscans, Capuchins, Carmelites—ice cream,
never before have the kids had such a choice of flavors,
never before have the Ten Commandments
been so cool in summer. I believe
when the holy family rested on their flight to Egypt,
in the desert heat, they had a little mystical lemon or orange ice,
before chocolate and vanilla crossed the unnamed Atlantic.
Let us pray, not for forgiveness, but for our just dessert.

Visiting Star

I woke at sunrise,
fed my dogs, Honey and Margie—
to the east a wall of books and windows,
a lawn, the trees in my family,
the donkeys and forest behind the hill.
Sunlight showed itself in,
passed the China butterflies on the window
so birds watch out, don't break their necks.
On the back of a green leather chair for guests
facing me in sunlight and shadow, a sunlit Star of David,
two large hand spans square.
I call to my wife to see the star
she first thinks I painted on the chair.
Soon she catches on—no falling star.
We searched the room and outside.
How did the star come to be?
Without explanation. None.
The star visited a few minutes, disappeared,
or became invisible. Why?
I wondered if it was *le bel aujourd'hui*
or a holiday some Jews celebrate.
Playing fair, I told myself: watch out for
a crucifix anywhere before which
contrition saves condemned souls—
watch in the forest for portraits of the Virgin,
the wheel of Dharma down the road
that teaches "save all living beings,"
when the moon is full a crescent moon
reflected on a wall or lake.

Watch for flying horses!
I read the news of commandments broken.
Thou shalt not kill.
I write between the lines
Thou shalt not steal
seventy-five years from the life of a child.
Next day, I found my Star of David
was a glass sun and star reflection of
a tinkling shimmering wind chime made in China.
A pleasing, godless today fills my study.

The Carpenter

i.

That boy who made the earth and stars had to learn
to make a chair in his earthly father's shop.
Above in the hip and valley of the rafters
held fast by joints his father cut
there is a haloed dove with outspread wings.
To the boy the workbench with its candle seemed
an altar, the tools offerings. That boy
could speak the languages of Babel. "Bevel"
he learned refers to an angle not cut-square.
At first he heard angle as angel.
He heard "take the angel directly from the work,
the only precaution being that
both stock and tongue be held tight to the work...
The boat builder bevel is most venerable."
The person of the dove shook head and halo
from side to side, vented a white splash
that smelled of water lilies on the boy's cheek and shoulder.
Then a whispering Third Voice filled the workshop.
"It's time to make an Ark to hold the Torah.
Learn the try-square, hammers and nails, veneers."
It was Friday afternoon, just before sunset.
The boy went to the steps of the synagogue.
He told the gathered doctors: "God commanded Moses
Build the Tabernacle of acacia wood, gave
exact dimensions, in cubits and hand-breadths."
The boy's mother called him:
"Carpenter, Yeshua, come to supper."

ii.

At night the boy returned to the workshop.
He shoplifted himself from the Holy Books
and the forbidden Greeks. He grinned:
a god deceived his wife Hera, who threw snakes
in the crib of the misbegotten babe Heracles
who strangled them. The boy giggled at the great
deeds of Heracles and his labors, that he only
became immortal after being burned alive.
In the sawdust Yeshua smelled forests,
he could tell cedar from pine, from oak, eucalyptus.
He saw the valleys of death and life.

With his father's tools he cut dovetails,
male and female angles, lapped dovetails
that show on one face but are concealed
on the other with lap and lip, secret dovetails
where the joint is entirely hidden.
The boy had spent a sad afternoon with the people.
Why were so many ears, eyes, and hearts deaf to him?
He told them it was written in Chronicles:
"The house of the Lord is filled with a cloud…
the Lord said he would dwell in the dark cloud."
The boy had never heard the word kristianos.
He saw his face in a pail of water, a cloudless sky.
He heard a cock crow, drunken Roman soldiers
laughing in the street. It was morning.

Drinking Song

It makes no difference if friends and family
are ashes thrown into the ocean,
or flesh and bone buried in holy ground,
their names barely attached. Awake or dreaming,
I see them as they were young and old, living
some other life, never in rags, never dressed to kill.
I don't trivialize the dead,
put them in a playground on a see-saw
or climbing a maze.
I remember their voices like
warped 78-turns-a-minute records—
stumbling voices.
I drink "to life!"
drinking a little from each glass "to death!"
because everything that is has death in it.

Look, the dead are school teachers,
they remember our names,
they grade us by number or letter;
they teach, "Fools, you don't know
how much more the half is than the whole."
The dead are trees. We are cut from their lumber.
And the dead are stars that no longer exist,
so far away their light is just reaching us.
Death is a doormat that says Welcome,
a good night's sleep, a handful of stones.
To a little death before I die! La petite mort!
Because the breast taken from the child
is a first death, I drink "to a nursing mother!"

and a first death the Christ child must have suffered.
I do not sing of phantom paradise
but offer a little phantom pleasure,
justice delayed—a hacksaw
for the phantom pain Ahab felt
after his severed leg was replaced by whalebone.
A hundred years! Bottoms up!

Letter to Dannie Abse

Doctor, I could have asked but never did
why weren't you a teacher or a drunk?
I could have asked you about your caring for
the wounded Nazi Luftwaffe Offizier.
Poet, you wrote love poems in your old age.

Jew, not by chance your son's name is David—
honors the psalmist and Saint Davy.
We celebrate spring at the same table,
suffer the same wintry fever.
In a pub called The Good Life the landlord serves
with every glass of joy a tankard of sorrow.

Husband, I never asked about your marriage,
it would have been asking why there's morning
and evening. Welshman, we first met at Hay-on-Wye.
You said, "The Welsh are a defeated people,
they identify with victims."

I send you brotherly love.
You don't need a brother, but I do.

A Kid in a "Record Crowd"

It was a little like what I feel now
walking around the City
remembering the old buildings
where new construction is going on.
It was a little like getting older.
I remember my fear as a child
being pushed by tens of thousands
at Yankee Stadium Memorial Day,
afraid of falling, being pushed over and squashed,
not being able to find my father,
some shouting, some singing in victory,
then packed in the subway back to Queens,
lucky American, far from the cattle cars,
the ovens, franks and mustard on my lips.

Jerusalem Wedding

to David Amichai

The dead poet,
father of the bridegroom,
invited the guests by printed invitation
that was placed, in love, by the son and his bride
on the father's grave the morning before the wedding.
The happy ghost of the father
attended the wedding, cried out
like Hamlet's father, "Remember me"—
but instead of asking for vengeance like the murdered king,
the five hundred guests
heard the poet's voice among the blessings.

Spring Poem for Christopher Middleton

1.

It's Monday, I phone. You answer, coughing, whisper:
"My doctor says two days and I'll be dead.
I'm afraid of falling off the bed into my grave"—
that means to me a couple of twists
of the screwdriver or monkey wrench
and you'll become unintelligibly human.

My mind is a waterbug. I write chatter… Life and death
are unhappy lovers. Is there a marriage,
is life the bride or bridegroom?
How many times can a father give the bride away?
Do life and death create a nation, like the marriage
of Fernando and Isabella--death Aragon, life Castille?
No reason, there are always the disasters of war.
Dear friend, *death is part of life* doesn't work for me.
I prefer *the end is part of the play.*

Actors and gentles, there is a change of decorum,
a grave eccentricity performed in an O.
It is winter. The sun is like a slum.
Without a bone, your frightened dog
already shakes at the stench
of your death. Without philosophy
he licks your face and feet
in hope of resurrection. A winter passion,
your life is disrobed before the public,
you are denied another Sabbath for no reason.
It should displease the Lord—this passing on
we know nothing of. I do not say the beads.
I pray there is a God of love who reads.

2.

Ten winter days have passed. I phone.
I'm certain telephones don't ring
in Heaven, Hell, or Purgatory.
You answer, "Hello . . . the crisis is over.
Now my neurosurgeon says I have some time,
a day or two, a month, you never know,
. . . my handwriting is very shaky." Hurrah,
it's March, there's reason to hope you'll see
Texas summer corn, roses in Westminster in April.
Soon, I'll send you this poem for a laugh.
Metaphor and reality have not come together.
I invented your good dog,
a gift to keep you from loneliness.

3.

(Is it better that the dead are buried
or go up in flames in clean clothes?)
In your poetry, you write under oath
not to treat as a thing of the mind
things that are of the mind only.
After their jealousy and lovemaking,
beauty and truth marry at the local registry,
take the vows of all religions,
or just have a long affair. I toast "To life!"
Christopher, brush away death by failing heart;
better Zeus, on a distant evening,
when you are surrounded by love,
ground you with a thunderbolt.
A hundred years!

Spoon

for Jane Freilicher

I was scribbling "Goya painted with a spoon" when I heard Jane died,
I knew enough not to be surprised but I was.
Saturn gnawed his sons without a place setting.
I never got over the Berliner Ensemble's *Mother Courage,*
when she screamed, "I bargained too much"
(for her murdered son's life).
The actress wore a wooden spoon as a broach.
Tongue tied, I kept "spoon." It is not a decoration.

In a daydream, I avow without reason
Jane Freilicher painted with a spoon—
potato fields, Watermill, pink mallow,
her early painting Leda and the Swan,
nothing we see—and with everyday palette knife,
brushes or late-invented forks,
useful for painting hydrangeas and eyelashes,
proof painters work like translators,
English into Chinese, everyday English words:
daylight, flower, woman, moon
are different in Ming, Tang, and Song:
different characters, different calligraphy.

She painted with a silver or oak spoon
ponds or stars, bones were oblongs and triangles,
nothing we see. She painted light,
mastered it, was mastered by it,
moved the world by "tipping the horizon up."
My honor: from a distance she painted
my house on Mecox Bay, my Corinthian columns,

my garden and sandspit
along the old Montauk road, my beach plums,
fireweed, roses of Sharon, day lilies, love
mostly washed out by hurricanes.
I say "my," but I never thought
I had good title to anything or anyone.
Then there was her battle of dreams
versus hallucinations, battles without a heroine,
the colors of fate, breathtaking, inevitable colors.
She would never forgive
those who think painting and poetry
function about the same as wallpaper.
Sometimes she painted small pictures
easily hidden from search parties
as Goya did, hiding from the Inquisition
because he painted nudes,
Protestant fields, Catholic fields, Jewish fields, like her.
She suffered the heresies of the Hamptons
where most painters of roses, whatever their personal faith,
and all poets, as such, are polytheists.
Again, she studied the many moods
of the sun and ocean through a window.
I studied Chinese at the Beijing railroad station,
eight thousand years or so of Chinese faces.
Every Chinese knows five cardinal relations:
ruler subject, father son, husband wife,
elder and younger brother, friend and friend.
I share the undiscovered country that begins
at the Southampton railroad station,

the beauty and color of Long Island
in the mist . . .
I sit shivering with the old-timers, gossiping
about the steam engines
from Penn Station to Montauk
100 years ago, faster than now, the island's
chestnut trees harvested for firewood,
the cemeteries, a little away from the railroad tracks,
cornflowers and poppies,
off Routes 114, 27, Springs Fireplace Road,
overloaded with painters,
I kiss my Yoricks. I knew them well.

*

Jane, we watched the pagan ocean
that holds bottom feeders
that thrive in fiery volcanic waters,
and birds that never come ashore.
Often we met at the beach, half-naked
barefooted or in sandals.
We knew where fifty-six swans nested,
that Long Island painters seldom painted
the night, or character. We chased whales,
saved wounded seals.
After an Atlantic hurricane, in our trees
with salt-drenched curled leaves,
thousands of fooled monarch butterflies gathered
on their way to Mexico.
We embraced 65 years ago—
not a long time for a redwood,
a long time for an oak or an elm.

The day you died,
I wish *ex cathedra*, Pope Francis said, "dogs go to heaven,"
so fawns, foxes, and rabbits aren't left behind.
You understood shadow.
At first look, you never painted sorrow.
You picked up stemless flowers, homeless
like beauties standing on street corners,
gorgeous juvenile delinquents.

Poem of the Pillow

1.

I believe love saves the world from heartbreak.
I'm learning to play the concrete harp.
I'm tired of traveling by my name only.
It is time for tears held back and washed away,
days that mean "yes" and nights that mean "no."
Look, the moon never disconsonant
lies down, sleeps under a bridge.
Still, when I am asleep, at breakfast,
reading a book or walking across a street
thinking I am far from eternal sloth, a God
for his comfort will push me out of sight.

2.

Veiled Fortuna, because knowing who you were,
I made you laugh and gave you pleasure
when you opened your mortal dressing gown,
give me proof that has no text—life everlasting
is to be loved at the moment of death.
Now my thoughts drift to a Japanese woodcut:
a sacred lake, a child's sailboat, the shore
a woman's open thighs, her gorgeous vulva.
At a distance, a flowering plum mouths a tall pine.
Deep within her leaves there is a poem of the pillow.

Happy 87th Birthday

to Willis

Years are numbered, as if they were the same,
some leap, some scythe-carriers are lame.
You know the date you were born
but nothing that happened for a couple of years
when you started remembering—an acorn—
you became an oak—forgot miracles. Your fears:
falling and fires—you knew love
before you knew the word. Mother's milk
holds many secrets, some cruelty and milk
of human kindness. What are you made *of*?
What are you *from*? Words different as silk
from linen and wool. I send a kiss and love
by email, modern love, not Adam's stuff.
We are *of* clay, and *from* porcelain.
Death is a volcano, we must not fall in.
From now on every day is Christmas.
Amor pesetas y tiempo para gastarlas.
I believe in original blessing, not original sin.

Letter to a Fish

I caught you and loved you when I was three
before I knew the word death—
it was a little like picking an apple off a tree.
At 20, I caught you, kissed you, and let you go.
You swam off like quicksilver.
The Greeks thought a little like that the world began.
You splashed and smacked your tail, made a rainbow.
Funny what drowns a man gives you breath.
Where are you, in ocean, brook, or river?
You suffer danger, but cannot weep as I can.
They say one God made the Holy books.
I offer Him my flies, spinners, feathered hooks—
not prayers. I swim with you in the great beneath,
to the headwaters of the unknown, in the hours
before dawn when fish and men exchange metaphors.

The Fish Answers

My school saw the Red Sea parted—you speak
to me only in North Sea everyday English
or Cape Cod American—why not ancient Greek?
I speak the languages of all those who fish
for me, and I speak Frog, Turtle, and Crocodile.
The waters are calm, come swim with me a while.
Look, the little fish will inherit the earth
and seas. Fish as you would have others fish for you!
Swallow the hook of happiness and mirth,
baited with poetry, the miraculous rescue.
I read drowned books. The Lord is many.
I heard this gossip in Long Island Sound:
Three days before he died, one Ezra Pound
told a friend, "Go with God, if you can stand the company."

Snowbound

I can't walk far or drive away.
I'm here, deep in snow.
Still, I can follow the heart
better than on a sunny day.
Snow, rain, and stars have a language
I've heard them speak,
beyond understanding, a language
they've written on earth from the start,
older than Chinese, Hebrew, or Greek,
indifferent to human weather
or where we gather.
I'm snowbound,
not sure if snow is prose—
ice, poetry—
or the other way around.
The winds live timelessly,
the weather comes and goes.
I adore a snow goddess
in her white drifting dress.

Rope

If I held a rope in my mouth,
you pulled and I pulled,
I would not enjoy it for long—proof
I'm not your dog.
If you pull my tongue with your teeth
I might find it fun a little while—
proof of strength, tug of war.
Then there is a tug of peace,
a long kiss when we pull together against death
that is the opposite of everything.

Silent Poem

I never took a vow of silence, but I am silent.
I walk thoughtlessly and thoughtfully through forests.
Sometimes I have nothing I want to say out loud.
I want my body alone to talk for me:
to touch, to hold, to love. My tongue can say a lot
without words. My hands have never prayed
or fingered holy tassels. My eyes, my ears, my nose
gossip about who I am, my nonsense.
I may be silent out of cleanliness,
respecting things unnamed, the simple truth
without words, beginnings without words,
silence I hear, silences I keep secret.
I confess I shout in fury like a woman scorned.
I am for beautiful madness, fair play,
reversals in social status,
like Don Quixote dedicating his quest
to Dulcinea, a kitchen wench. I assuage
the ludicrous monsters of eternal life—
a three-legged priest.

Signifier

Ill-mannered, it might have been a death,
a sudden inhaling and exhaling, something before,
after, or during speech, not a word,
nothing to do with discourse, not a breath,
yet a blessing to a drowning man. A blessing
to the infant after the mother's breast.
I sing not of the wrath of Achilles
but of thin air and effect, a kind of aftertaste
that may be veiled, suppressed with a finger
to the lips, a sign of a certain changing, as water changes,
not tide, not pulse, not from the heart at all,
but a sign of life, a mumble within the body,
invisible, unintelligible, comic perhaps,
a poor, strutting player, signifying something,
unpersuasive, possessing tone, pitch, distantly
related to the yawn, the ah, without ecstasy,
no more important than this Pounding
base bass voice.

Pacemaker

1.

I take no pleasure in saying
I'm not a pacemaker or stallion on a dead run,
part of my history,
without a halter, when I was 23,
I pulled a wagon
from 10 Quai Voltaire,
desk, books, and pretty dresses,
to 13 bis Rue de Tournon.
I stir the summer dust:
a lady said she heard my heart
beating across the room.

2.

Years past, sometimes on a dead run, a dead walk,
I fainted like a Victorian girl.
Now, I wear a pacemaker connected to my heart
by reins and wires that protect my heart from beating
37 irregular beats per minute.
Yesterday, tomorrow, today
my heart is fixed.
My pulse, andante, seldom allegro,
continues with its versification.
Lady with the sweet countenance of a soup spoon,
lead my heart through enjambment, spondaic,
iambic syllable count, in and out of schemes,
to the last syllable of my heartbeat,
awake and asleep in praise.

Granite

When I was five I loved climbing a granite boulder,
almost a mountain. I kissed it and grown-ups laughed.
Standing on top, almost naked,
I could see to the other side of the lake,
the lily-pads and forests. I felt immortal.
My father spent that summer
in Venice and Vienna.

I remember an August storm, I was in the clouds
surrounded by my thunder, lightning, and rain.
I loved that, but I lost my footing,
slipped down, tore the skin off my back.
I still have the scars and the granite dust
in the scars under my shirt.

Today I returned to the lake,
paddled along the shore. I had to trespass,
but I found my granite boulder.
I kissed her again.
Who else can I kiss that I kissed when I was five?
I kissed the flowers in her mortal crevices.
Does she dream she is a dancer, alabaster?
I held my boulder close as I could.

Sunset—Night

Hell

—thanks to George Herbert's "Heaven"

O who shall show me such suffering?
Echo.   Ring.
You, Echo, immortal clown all men know.
Echo.   No.
Still in the mountains don't you die away?
Echo.   Way.
I wept when the King of Jews came harrowing.
Echo.   Rowing.
Prophets of slavery and war I applaud:
Echo.   Laud.
those who celebrate Christmas
Echo.   Mass.
by first cutting down a tree
Echo.   Tree.
rather than planting an evergreen.
Echo.   Green.
To celebrate peace on earth
Echo.   Earth.
I take gifts to the rich then sing
Echo.   Sing.
Come all ye faithful…
Echo.   Full.
Tell me what is the supreme horror?
Echo.   Or.
The truth, God the clown created us
Echo.   Us.
for laughter not for praise that he abhors.
Echo.   Whores.
The business of the soul is live for profits.
Echo.   Fits.

Onward indifference! Starvation! Fiery justice!
Echo.   Ice.
A touch of kindness makes the devil fart.
Echo.   Art.

I Sit Much with My Dog

When I write at home my dog is not far off.
When I read poems aloud, mine or others',
I sometimes scare him. If I had a house I would
let him outside on such occasions,
but in my apartment, he's stuck with me.
My dog, alas, is stuck with poetry,
as I am. I read a poem
that is a hearty call in the night.
My dog becomes morbid. I think
I'm getting an inch closer to God.
My dog thinks I'm angry at him,
doesn't know what to do, or what to stop doing.
He just looks up and can't help it.
I call him over in the middle of my reading,
reassure him that I am still my smelly self,
but there is something changed between us.
As soon as I begin to read out loud, he thinks
something's wrong, or something's about to happen.
Sancho, if I knew how, I'd write you a dog poem.
Somehow I know there is something
I can never make up to you,
that sniffing after beauty I terrorize you.

Cautionary Tale

I said we don't know what your 63-year-old
schizophrenic son may do with his history:
he made fires in hospitals, called 911 "for company,"
cut himself, jumped out windows,
leaving behind feces in dresser drawers,
in and under the bed. Dreadful etceteras.
Mostly silent, he talks sweetly to dogs
he calls by dead dogs' names.
You said, "It snowed a foot yesterday
doesn't mean it will snow today."
I didn't say, "No snowfall ever played the piano."
We both know John Little played Bach on the piano,
went home on a weekend, killed his mother and father.
I remember, for no reason, when I was sweet and 20,
when the snow was deep in the city,
the streets at night almost empty,
I climbed the snowdrifts and sang arias from *The Magic Flute*,
recited lines from *Hamlet* and Yeats, Hart Crane.
Truth is, a good blizzard with drifts two meters high
gave me the opportunity to speak to the gods.
Snow-blind, I wish I could take your hand,
I insist I can find the way through the blizzard of madness
down the road to the mailbox.
I will not crawl into a schizophrenic cage
with you and His Majesty.

Song of Jerusalem Neighbors

What proves I am not your enemy?
Our dogs fight. Your music gets in my hair,
you think my voice has a bad odor.
Your laundry hanging or drying on the ground
looks like mine. My prayer shawl is invisible,
I'll be buried in it—your Islamic robe
covers you with clouds. I look at your wife's red bra,
you look at my wife's black lace panties.
We each have handkerchiefs for weeping.
We are suspicious of cans and pots
of geraniums, blue and pink anemones.
Who brought 613 laws to the Sinai,
red ants? I don't gloat when it rains
only on my side of the barbed wire.
When I broke my arm I thought
something in your eye twisted it.
I thought your baby was beautiful—
I don't want her to kill anybody.
You say, "Unless I get to you first. This is
middle-class donkey shit."
Neither of us curses in his own language.
Jehovah and Allah are lollipops
for the motherfuckers who find war
sexually attractive.

Affluent Reader

to Oliver Sacks

I borrowed a basket of grapes, I paid back in wine.
I borrowed a pail of milk, I paid my debt in Gorgonzola.
I borrowed my life, I tried to pay back in poetry:
an autumn breeze blew my poems away—
dry leaves, *insufficient funds.*
I'm still in debt for my life.
God is a lender, has a pawnshop,
hangs out the sun and moon, his sign.
He is in business 'round the clock:
I receive summons after summons
often in the middle of the night
demanding payment dollar for dollar,
for every year every minute and heartbeat
for every penny of my life—my death
plus interest: usurious eternity.

The American Dream

Stuck in my suburban flesh and marrow,
the static news of mass murder, Blitz, burning ghettos . . .
At fifteen I made love in deep snow
in moonlight. I did not go all the way,
betraying myself, Claire McGill and poetry.
She was seventeen half naked used her tongue.
It would have been a miracle, my first time,
not hers. Is she alive, does she remember?
I raved about Lorca and Rimbaud.
It would not be long. I learned to kill before I learned to rhyme.

I limp into her chamber, a goat with old horns.
I think she will recognize my ghost, young,
able to make her laugh, among the coterie
of ghosts she did it with, while I cavorted
with Maria de las Nieves, Eros of the snow,
obeyed the commandment Djuna Barnes
gave me when I was 27, waving goodbye
with her walking stick, "Follow the heart, follow the heart!"

My heart led me to illusion, but it didn't lie.
I was manned, boyed, womaned and girled.
I learned to trust trees, blind trees, lonely trees,
forests. I rely on their wisdom—as I will after I die.
Today a child asked me, "How much love is in a kiss?"
I said: "I don't know." She said, "The whole world."

No Tear Is Commonplace

No tear is commonplace.
The prophet said,
"Woman is the pupil of the eye."
All beauty
comes from God,
butterflies
fly from and to God one by one
and to the forests of Michoacán
where Mexicans nearby make
Jesus Christ
from parrot feathers
and wings of hummingbirds.
You can hold such a God
against your cheek,
then you are as if
under a wing,
a firstling,
warm and comforted.

December 8

May these words serve as a crescent moon:
in Barcelona 58 years ago today
I saw on the front page of *La Vanguardia*
beside the main altar of the cathedral
two polished cannons blessed by the Archbishop
in the name of Saint Barbara, patron
of Generalissimo Franco's artillery
on this day set aside to celebrate
the Immaculate Conception.

Today in a Greek gallery off 5th Avenue
I saw Aphrodite blinded by a Christian,
a cross chiseled into her eyes and forehead.
Outside in a hard rain, Christmas season,
no taxis. I was chased by the wind
through the open door of Saint Patrick's Cathedral.
Up since 4, I slept in the false Gothic darkness.
A bell announcing the Holy Spirit woke me
to a mass celebrating the Immaculate Conception.
Can a Jew by chance receive a little touch of absolution—
like a touch of a painter's brush
like a little touch of King Harry
visiting his troops in the night before Agincourt?
I have prayers put in my head
like paper prayers in the cracks of the wailing wall.
The heart has reason, reason does not know.

Elegy for the Poet Reetika Vazirani and Her Child

If life were just, for strangling her two-year-old child
before murdering herself, my dear friend
would be sentenced to life at hard labor:
fifty lines a day before she sleeps
in a bare room with a good library and her son's guitar.
When will she have a change of heart,
when will she take pity on those who love her,
when will the terror she caused her child no longer appear in the sky?
The sun and moon hang around absolutely without conscience.

Notices

Once an Irishman in his coffin
had to be wrapped from foot to chin
in English wool, not Irish linen.
I saw this notice: "Some striped scars on his back,
runaway slave stole himself, calls himself Jack."

Rival

You were always a great one with the ladies.
Toward the end you only wanted to suck
a piece of ice. Embracing no one
you could not be embraced. No one
was allowed in the room.
I watched through the glass.
A pretty nurse was washing
your last blood and excrement.
I swear she was singing.

SM

With spray can paint,
I illuminate my name
on the subway cars and handball courts,
in the public school yards of New York,
S M
written in sky-above-the-ocean-blue,
surrounded by a valentine splash
of red and white, not for Spiritus Mundi,
but for a life and death, part al fresco
part catacomb,
against the city fathers
who have made a crime of signaling
with paint to passengers and pedestrians.
For the ghetto population of my city
I spray my name
with those who stand for a public art.
In secret if I must
and wearing sneakers, I sign with those
who have signed for me.

Mocking Gods

Lost in the library of Alexandria, proof
Selene the moon goddess mocked Apollo
her sun god twin, each mocking the other
about mortal offsprings—
off-summers, off-autumns, off-winters.
More than "divine," an inadequate human word
for speaking about gods, all words
are mostly useless. A messenger whispered,
"That's why prayers and sacrifice were invented."
Without Apollo, simple daylight, music
and poetry, nothing on earth lives.
Beautiful beyond belief, Selene spent years
in front of her mirrors, the oceans,
so close to the earth, she said the breathing
of humans and animals sometimes kept her awake.
Crashing a feast of the gods, a mortal boy
in rapture surrendered to Selene,
who gave birth to another moonchild.
Apollo and other gods remembered
Selene had fifty daughters with Endymion.

What fools call "twenty years" passed,
the moonchild, male or female,
had a lover—pity the darling who held close
a celestial body, equally at home
on earth or sky—half a night or day,
especially since that moonchild in turn
might have a child, more mortal now
than half moon, but still mooning,
playing in the park among other children
with everyday faces.

Put the case: Apollo and a mortal beauty
could have twins that brighten the darkest room
or forest, who fight as brothers and sisters
to prove who is father or mother's favorite—
neither so naughty to challenge Apollo at music.
At night, the children would weep for their father,
busy with godly affairs.
The poor mortal mother mostly in the kitchen
preparing meals, finally insisted on her right
to be Jew, Christian, or Muslim
or better still, she said to the sun god, "all three!"

Today I heard the sun laugh, I swear I heard
happy thunder, thunder without anger or lightning,
and the moon laughing like Sarah
hiding behind a cloud's curtain.

Now

I am just a has been and a will be.
What *is* right now that is the question.
My fool says I should learn from today's clouds:
"The verb 'to be' is English lightning—
lightning and thunder are happily married,
their vows are storms. Now, now, Uncle,
the plural is sweet company, fair weather,
then there is the conjugation, we are, they are,
the all or none, till 'everybody' is singular again."
Fool, my fly is open, needs to be buttoned.

I enjoy the soufflé of *la vague* and *le vague,*
the feminine "wave" and masculine "indefinite."
I relish the English Christmas pudd
of nouns made into verbs and verbs into nouns.
Since childhood I've been forested,
lost in the woods of conditional verbs,
lost in the woulds, what should I do
left wandering and wondering
where is the golden fool, the sun?
The forests one summer, inflamed by false gods,
left charcoal barrens that nourish the soil.
The trees will grow another time,
a time for rhyme, and a time to run out of time—
the hours around the clock
like hyenas around a carcass.

Tightrope Walking

Tightrope walkers know
they must look at the wire a few paces ahead,
never at their feet.
Walking the high wire of poetry
you have to look at your feet,
while you can't help keeping track
of clouds moving carefully,
a lost redwing blackbird inside the tent
trying to get out,
a poet's son, a French acrobat,
wire behind you, the net below,
a pretty face in the crowd, cash receipts.
All this worthless information
does not make a poem.
It's as hard as selling old underwear
to write a poem about nothing.

Smiles

I argued with a dear friend, a psychiatrist
who didn't think dogs smile and dream.
I told him I thought butterflies, frogs and dogs dream
and smile—that the whole Bronx Zoo is like me,
but I don't think every Greyhound bus,
cheese, beggarman and thief is named Stanley.
I've seen trees smiling, dreaming, kissing and kissed.
I don't think the world is a mirror made by Jesus,
rather sooner or later, like Columbus,
every old sailor sees a mermaid, that Jesus
smiled and dreamed like us, and Judas
had a dog that smiled and dreamed like us.
My good dog Bozo ran wild with my shoes.
Because I sleep and dream old news,
secrets I keep from myself, I smile in deceit,
while my dog smiles, mounts a wolf at my feet.

A Metaphoric Trap Sprung

Poets, step carefully, your foot, eye, ear, love
may be caught in a metaphoric trap,
like the bear's severed foot.
Crying out or laughing is no use,
the only release is writing it off.
You don't escape fatally wounded,
you can't lick the blood away.
Learning languages helps—take *work*,
whose Chinese character includes a hand.
Too heartbroken to talk?
Every muse has eight sisters.
Where love is
or has been—words,
words spoken while making love
become flesh.

Mind

They come to mind, not of my choosing,
in several languages, women I loved,
the living and the dead, in beds here and there,
in different countries.
I remember waiting in doorways endlessly
when it seemed all love was safely abed.
Truth is, love will never come back to me from "mind"—
in my English, neuter, without gender.

Christmas 2014

Nothing I say will change anything.
I am dismayed on Christmas day.
There's sickness in my house,
almost a black Christmas.
Deep in a snowdrift, I make myself a snowmother,
the Virgin, put a snow savior in her arms.
One day, He will melt in her arms and she in His,
they will wake up a little unresurrected pond
that will fill with waterlilies in spring
if I have anything to say about it,
but I have nothing to say about it.
Bring on the snapping turtles and leaches
evergreens, bristlecones,
that may live a thousand years.
I trust trees, I have faith in butterflies and poets,
who these days and nights live days and nights.
How can God be a cannibal and a good guy?
A High Mass sings the answers to all questions.
This spring, I will join the wise young
dancing around a maypole, undismayed.

2 AM

Sola una cosa tiene mala el sueño, según he oído decir,
y es que se parece a la muerte, pues de un dormido a un
muerto hay muy poca diferencia.
                    —*Sancho Panza*

It is 2 AM. I need to rest, sleep.
I risk being entertained by the clown of death
at a dream circus, I see half his face—
white and red likeness doesn't frighten me.
I am a lie-down comedian.
It is 2 AM. Among my last thoughts:
my wife's operable cancer... Marianne Moore in 1916
wore her red hair in braids... I don't want the clown
to wash his face, change into my street clothes.
My wife has a cancerous node.
St. Teresa read books on chivalry.
At a tender age, she and her brother agreed
to run off to the Moors' country, beg their bread
for love of God, to reach heaven beheaded.
At supper, an Avila spring or two before,
St. Teresa answered the first question,
"How is this night different from all other nights?"
It is 2 AM. Joy! Joy! William Carlos Williams
saw more than 2,000 babies pulled through
one way or another into the world. It is 2 AM.
I sat in at his poorly attended funeral
in Rutherford: no poets I recognized,
no words I remember, family, sons, Fanny,
scattered in the pews mostly old pretty ladies.

I must have fallen into eternity.
The telephone did not ring
but I was on the phone with Charlie Williams.
He was going to see Dylan Thomas.
I said I'd fly over. We'd go together.
Dylan was alive, no question.
Charlie was in Paris, did not have cancer,
no question. We would just have a good time.

Thank God for pleasant dreams.
It never crossed my mind to talk about God
with Dylan, but when we were coming downtown
in a taxi from the Academy with Carl Sandburg,
64 years ago, Dylan played God
receiving T.S. Eliot in heaven: "Come in.
I've read your Four Quartets."
Dylan loved the stranger, wrote ". . . in praise of God,"
said he'd be "a damned fool" if he didn't.

*

Back from my entertainments, I woke up.
Half asleep, I was in bed with my wife
and Margie my dog, named after my mother.
I saw lady sunrise, naked, with all her troubles
come into the bedroom past the apple tree.
The lights of an automobile down the road
brought me to my senses. I never served time
in an overcrowded prison, shackled to no labor.
I never complained about the weather.
There are other places, names, and matters

I do not care to remember.
I read in Don Quixote there's an old ballad
that says King Rodrigo, alive and kicking
in a tomb filled with reptiles and vermin,
said in a low and mournful voice,

"They're eating me, they're eating me
in the place where I most sinned."
Sancho did not think the most sinful place
was the brain, the mind. He did not remember
that Jesus Christ said thinking something evil
was the same as doing it. Certainly, the squire knew
we think of doing unto others more evil than we do,
he heard the devil hides behind the cross.

Fathers

1.

A friend told me Jesus said,

"Go out into the fields to find your real mothers and fathers."
I thought somehow I'd done that
since I really had two fathers, none heavenly,
a subject difficult for me to talk about.
I am confused—straighten me out.
I am old and difficult under the apple boughs.
I have planted more apple trees than I can remember.

I've searched but I cannot find a text that reveals
when or how Christ's earthly father died.
I see it was from His not-blood-father, Joseph,
that Jesus was begot from patriarchs and kings—
soon the innocents were slaughtered, Joseph
took flight with the Virgin and child to Egypt
by donkey that would not eat sacred manger hay,
the beast said to have prayed when they rested.

Later, the way things happen, Joseph corrected
Aramaic speaking Jesus' Hebrew,
taught Him Torah, morning prayer, perhaps to skip
a stone out to sea. Did Joseph teach his carpenter Son
what the boy taught the rabbis? Holy riddle.
Surely Jesus sang prayers in synagogue
and at home with windows open, stopped traffic
when he sang everyday love songs.
We know Joseph had four sons of his own blood.
He compounded with his wife,

so he and Mary kissed carnally, perhaps on the Sabbath:
he must have loved her smell, touch, taste—her breasts
from which Jesus took the milk of human kindness.
His four younger brothers sucked the same nipples.

Of course Jesus, with His knowledge and direction
of everything that happens, was, is, never jealous.
His jealousy, the devil's suggestion.

No news that his Son embraced him when Joseph
was on his deathbed dying a happy death—
He might have brought Joseph a cup of hot chocolate
the dying in Mexico who worshipped snakes
took comfort from.
Chocolate had not yet come to Rome or Jerusalem.
Alas, Joseph is not buried beside his wife in Ephesus.
John the Divine is buried a few steps from Her tomb;
a stone's throw away is the Temple of Artemis,
the virgin huntress-goddess, sister of Apollo.
The way things happen, Mary visited the Greek temple
one of the seven wonders, changed by wars into Roman.

     2.

I know a tree the shape of five question marks
when? how? why? which? where?
every word forbidden fruit.
A summer rain takes over my life
then simply abandons me.
I had a father whom most held in high regard
he deserved. Others called him evil.
My sister and I independently
were reminded of our father we called "father"

when we saw a newspaper photograph
of the decade's most famous murderer.
My mother said father was always angry,
but I had a godfather, her brother, a doctor,
beside whom for me, Gabriel, Rafael, Elijah,
and all the gods were pimps.
As a child I had to be forced to eat an apple.
I have never bit an apple since I left my father's house,
still I believe the apple does not fall far from the tree.

Psalm

God of paper and writing. God of first and last drafts,
God of dislikes, God of everyday occasions—
He is not my servant, does not work for tips.
Under the dome of the Roman Pantheon,
God in three persons carries a cross on his back
as an aging centaur, hands bound behind his back, carries Eros.
Chinese God of examinations: bloodwork, biopsy,
urine analysis, grant me the grade of *fair* in the study of dark holes,
fair in anus, self-knowledge, and the leaves of the vagina
like the pages of a book in the vision of Ezekiel.
May I also open my mouth and read the book by eating it,
swallow its meaning. My Shepherd, let me continue to just pass
in the army of the living,
keep me from the ranks of the excellent dead.
It's true I worshipped Aphrodite
who has driven me off with her slipper
after my worst ways pleased her.
I make noise for the Lord.
My Shepherd, I want, I want, I want.

The Perfect Democracy

I come close to the perfect democracy
a poet called "the kingdom of death."
I was created and I will die free and equal.
My soul was born on the North Atlantic
between Lithuania and Philadelphia,
city of brotherly love. I don't remember but surely
my heart can't forget being nursed, then rocked
by my mother and the Atlantic Ocean. (What a first nanny.)
These days almost everyone's a landlover,
who never spent days or weeks
looking out at nothing but endless ocean and horizon.
How can such a landlover know who he or she is
in the world and universe?

Almost everyone, when you cross the little brook
between life and death,
you will enter the democratic halls of death,
parliaments, congress, la Chambre des Députés,
take your seats before the Speaker, you will be
called to order, shrouded in your Sunday best,
perhaps a winding sheet or prayer shawl,
or you may sit, entombed, like the old Tatars,
with pipe, tobacco, and live dog;
some will have a clear view through the open roof
to the Sun and Moon, others, under the merciful eyes
of Jesus or Jehovah or both, are asleep in the Commons.
Most are "officer's mess" for batallions of maggots.
Few rest in peace. Some debating good citizens
hold hell is simply a cleptocracy, the dead
are cleaned out, without a penny's worth of anything.
Others mutter they are "never dead, not even past."

Mr. Speaker:
I salute the eight black constituents
to the Assemblée Nationale,
in the valley with the Jews who were included
in the Declaration of the Rights of Man
thanks to one vote, now a skinless finger.
Everyone knows his or her deathday.
No one sings "Happy deathday to you"
except a few still drunk on life.
Morning. A dog seems to rest its head
on smoke that smells human.
The cock calls the role. The nays have it.

O landlovers, I wish I could bring you shipboard,
surround you with blue, purple, white,
black and mountainous turquoise breakers,
bring you to their meaning and incomprehensibility,
to see what is near and beyond.
A few stand and pray
on the floor or alone in the coatrooms,
a congregation of pure Oversouls,
the odd murderer with nothing to do.

Landlover,
you may be a farmer or a gardener, bless you,
but just between you, me and the buttercups,
the ocean is coming. Question time:
Mr. Speaker, in your democracy,
are there any little deaths after death, *withouts*:
no need to have supper late or early,
no lovemaking, no music? Will I be a listener,
may I play a God-made instrument?

Surely democratic God arranges for birdsong,
winds praying in trees.

I'm filibustering. Does God eat?
I hear someone say God is a vegetarian,
another is certain God eats meat.
For centuries the best cuts were set aside for Gods.
Surely lambs were and are not sacrificed without reason.
Then God eats and, since we are made in God's image,
He defecates, urinates, wipes Himself clean.
God coughs and farts, is our Farter who art in Heaven.
I'm the Devil, you say! No, in the shadow cabinet
I'm the minister of parables. Every school child knows
Isis and other Gods of the dead are marble or bronze.
I'm trying to vote death out of office—
I say to the free man who praises his God,
"Without death, anarchy. Is God and his 42 names
protected by flights of angels, his Mom?"

The Lord swims in all oceans,
plays a kind of tag with jellyfish and whales,
He does not forget the least of the newborn.
His hand runs through, blesses many kinds of spawn.
I'm happy to have been born on the Atlantic,
my useful afterbirth thrown overboard.

In bedroom slippers, I tap-dance
up and down the stairs, hold onto the rail,
my pulse once a household member, now a guest,
cannot overstay his or her welcome.
My pulse cannot overstay his or her welcome.

The Gambler

Older, I gamble with one die,
risk rolling a one-eyed snake.
I hedge my bets with the verb "to die."
The chances are I'll die some daybreak,
I prefer after breakfast and a cup of coffee
to get me through the day. It would be nice
to read again *The Gambler* of Dostoyevski,
to play with God, but "God does not roll dice,"
flip coins—heads damnation, tails grace.
"Love the stranger" trumps where the true cross is.
He cheers for peace, not war, in a horse race,
although they are both His horses,
He collects His winnings and takes His losses.

Mercy's a wild card.
Now I play numbers with fallen angels.
(God knows what the Devil feels.)
The Lord will not settle for a little human regard.
His new-fangled messengers with smart-phones
text the laws, take selfies, see fire and brimstone.
I cheat at cards Yahweh deals.

Stuffed with flesh, blood, and bones,
I don't applaud any God. I lift my cap,
kick off my shoes, drop a coin in the box and clap.
I see a skyscraper as a gravestone.
Walking in New York City, forgetting is hard.
There is some reason to suppose the sap
of trees will outlast human blood by mishap.
The world shoots craps. I bet, no matter how winds fly,
a kiss will keep the world from hate, by and by.

It began, midnight. It was 1956,
I arrived in Nice by train
far from the Tiber and River Styx.
Tenth of August, no beds, with Djuna my dog,
I slept in a Hotel Negresco beach chair,
Djuna on colored stones, under my chair.
Storm clouds covered the stars.
We went into a casino to escape the rain.
Djuna died a Socialist wolf in Fascist Spain.
I still grieve for my Trastevere dog,
like a child. I'm left to speak the prologue.

But pardon, it is my wish
to honor the language. I salute the verb "to die,"
its sound and meaning from Middle English.
I play with sounds, with I and eye,
homonym-roulette: morning dew,
there's do unto others and Devil his due.
Rien ne vas plus. For those slated to die,
a shell game: where?, when?, why?.
Given time, all is vanity,
the Good Shepherd will lead the universe to slaughter.
Baa, baa, baa . . . I put my money on last laughter:
there are many more stars in the day and night sky
than there are words in English.
My words contain dark matter,
invisible gravity, water dripping from the tap—
I bet my life. I'd like to catch a fish
that's been swimming in the Thames since English.
I've caught Death, the rat, in my mousetrap—
Augustine's sermon 261. No,
I take Death into the woods and let him go.

Eclipse

A Rose

How can you run about
two minutes after you are born?
Be a horse, then you can discover
a valley, the taste of a mare's nipple,
your coat moist with her 3-year-old blood.
In a dream set partly in a horse barn,
greenhouse, outdoors classroom, I thought
universe after universe is not *here*,
is out there, out there, there, there,
there, still going . . .
Here and a rose are within my reach,
visible without wise instruments.
Our earth and sun don't matter an onion
to dark matter, places without address.
Justice is not done in the universe,
where the only evidence admissible is invisible
or with sweet deceiving countenance.
If all the world's a stage, the players have stage fright.
Ding dong, the final doorbell is ringing.
(In Middle Scottish "ding" means worthy.)
Mr. Trouble won't take his finger off
the button. I'm here, unmetaphorical.
No friend or Eurydice is like any other,
lost friends sometimes come as visitations.
Still I take up with string theory
or the rose-by-any-other-rose theory
that holds water.

A bee flew into a rose,
found darkness and silence there,
flew into another rose and another,
then bang, fires, everything.
Gravity and darkness are not dreary.
Mathematicians are heroes
who give meaning to numbers,
a wilderness of zeroes.
The thing about the cosmos
is what we cannot see is beautiful.
Not *I, you* and *me* is what I want to say.
My calling card is the periodic table.
I am thorium, the 90th element,
silvery and black.
Protons, the cosmos, black holes,
white dwarfs are never gross.
Soon after the invention of the present tense
there was comparative and superlative,
so off we went to war. We breathe in and out:
the simple past came just like that.

We believed, needed to pray, invented talk,
writing to keep accounts,
although greeting by smelling, whining,
crying, howling, served us well.
We could say *please, thank you, good morning*
and *good night, I love you*, without a word.
A child asked me a question: "Back at the start,
bang!, cruel, kind, or no heart?"

Album

Among family photos,
a school of smiling rainbow trout.
A magician uncle explained:
they swam across the ocean
although they were freshwater fish,
not saltwater fish. Our good fish family
studied hard underwater and learned
the scrolls, the shelves, the sudden drops.
They were taught to watch out
for sturgeon, salmon, striped bass
coming up river, some to die,
others laid eggs, then returned to the ocean.
My cousin looked for an underwater Bible
in the lily pads but never found it,
saw turtles as big as automobile tires,
but he kept looking, breaking water for heaven's sake.
Lucky he had eyes that saw in a full circle
not just straight ahead, so he did better.
They had a Watchman fish, an old fish,
too old to fertilize eggs,
every scale thick as a windscreen,
he watched for lone fish returning from war.
Somehow they became human.
They would rather be buried
than thrown overboard into any puddle.

Mr. Trouble

Whatever the season
I add and subtract days and weeks.
I was with my dogs in the park,
I met Monsieur Troublé,
"Mr. Trouble," laughing.
"What are you laughing at?" I asked.
He spake thus: "I've read you.
I grant every birth is a nativity, holy.
Love, perhaps simply befriending,
is the answer in a world
where looking at something changes it.
Yes, eyes change the world."
"No, no," a passing angel said, *"Ave Maria*
gratia plena, Dominus tecum—
words in the Virgin's ear gave her a Son."
I said, "Then the nose, smelling changes the world.
Tasting, barely touching or lovemaking changes the world."
"Nobody is speaking for the ocean," Mr. Trouble said.

I offered: Moonlight is the traveler
and there was a full moon—
moon, mothered by winter, mothered by spring.
Day goes where night was,
after a long time I go about as music—
let's say that's what the good life is,
carrying a tune.
Moonlight sees what daylight does.
"Monkey sees," Mr. Trouble said.
"Nobody is speaking for the ocean."

My Mother's Memorial Day

May 19th, a sleepless night,
thirty-six years after the ocean stopped swimming,
I didn't light a candle. I wrote a letter
to my mother, put a daisy in an envelope,
mailed it express, addressed "to far places."
The letter came back stamped *Return to sender.*
Nobody is speaking for the ocean.

Far back as I remember,
I saw my naked mother,
the ocean swimming endlessly, wonder full.
I did not know the Chinese say "woman is half the sky";
I thought my mother was half ocean, half firmament.
From time to time I overheard I harmed her forever.
They did not blame me. Still, my birth was a sin
like no other. It prisoned me.
I wished I was born from an egg
like a pigeon. I could not say "I'm sorry"
for what I was not allowed to know.
I believed my sin belonged only to me—
not one of the look-alikes forbidden by commandments.
I heard of penance, mine was simply crying.

At nine, I wanted to be a farmer.
I marveled at planting seeds, watching
things grow, and I wanted to be a priest
so I could hear confession, secret stories.
I could do nothing right.
To kiss was to make it "all better."

I was not a child walking in sand
with a pail and shovel looking out
at the swimming ocean. On the island of Rhodes,
on a Hellenistic street the Colossus protected,
in a celebration after a Greek revolution,
I was shot in the leg by a ricocheting bullet.
I swallowed the Acropolis,
a kind of Eucharist.
It never passed through my intestines.

Even so, life was an apparatus belonging to the city.
Life cleared streets, plowed snow, collected garbage,
is related to an ambulance, elevated trains.
It only made sense when I saw a field of wildflowers.
It took time before I took my time
reaching for what really was, is.
What is not   still is
my more than occasional companion.

Alexander Fu Musing

The truth is I don't know the days of the week.
I can't tell time.
I have lived a summer,
a fall, a winter, an April, a May,
which I say because words are put in my mouth
because you-know-who is trying to sell something.
My mother rocks me to sleep, singing
a Chinese lullaby about crickets playing.
It's not easy to know so little,
but I wake to wonder, I touch wonder,
I play with wonder.
I smile at wonder.
I cry when wonder is taken from me.

To Alexander Who Wants to Be a Cosmologist

September 27th and 28th, two dark rainy days.
Alex was shivering, crying for no reason.
Embraced, he sobbed. It was for lack of summer.
He thought summer was longer.
"It's cold. It's already autumn."
I told him, "You simply must learn to love
autumn, winter, and spring.
We are all star children, made of the stuff of stars.
Don't cry, we are living in the golden age of stars."

To Alexander Fu on His Beginning and 13th Birthday

Cut from your mother, there was a first heartache,
a loneliness before your first peek
at the world, your mother's hand was a comb
for your proud hair, fresh from the womb—
born at night, you and moonlight tipped the scale
a 6lb 8oz miracle,
a sky-kicking son
born to Chinese obligation
but already American.
You were a human flower, a pink carnation.
You were not fed by sunlight and rain.
You sucked the wise milk of Han.

Your first stop, the Riverdale station,
a stuffed lion and meditation.
Out of PS 24, you will become
a full Alexander moon over the trees
before you're done. It would not please
your mother to have a moon god for a son.
She would prefer you had the grace
to be mortal, to make the world a better place.
There is a lesson in your grandmother's face:
do not forget the Way
of your ancestors. Make a wise wish
on your 13th birthday, seize the day
from history and geography.
If you lead, you will not lose the Way,
in your family's good company
where wisdom is common as a sunfish,
protected from poisonous snakes by calligraphy:

paintings of many as the few, the few as many.
You already dine on a gluten-free dish
of some dead old King's English.
In your heart, keep Fu
before Alexander and do
unto others as you would have others do
unto you.

Children's Song

"I wish I was two dogs, then I could play with me."
I am King and Queeny,
I could chase two red squirrels up a tree,
rule a kingdom on my bed,
play very alive and very dead,
question and answer, sniffing dialogue,
play good dog, bad dog,
bark and laugh
with bull, cow, and calf,
answer a moo with bark bark,
have sweet company in the dark,
play two St. Bernards in the snow,
two Chihuahuas in Mexico,
a Bloodhound and Labrador,
till Papa, hands on hips,
says, *Quiet! Quiet!*, stands at the door
while I, with my two tongues, lick my lips.
I like dog biscuits, fish and chips.
I could go to bed late and early,
I could eat a bone, one, two, three,
and never be lonely, never be lonely.

Birthday Wishes

Lovers of birthdays,
he had 99 years.
The usual toast, "a hundred years!"
would be a curse
so they gave him
a basket of Georgia peaches,
the gift of a photo:
a woman reclining naked,
her tongue showing a little,
a handkerchief, with her hair
body odor and breath.
He and his guests
will celebrate his birthday
until there are no birthdays
anymore. Lovers of birthdays,
may circumstance, fate
bring him and you
a happier love-death
than an ancient death I recall:
Achilles, his face masked
behind a copper helmet,
slays Penthesilea
Queen of the Amazons,
as she dies, they fall in love…
Lovers of birthdays,
honest readers,
there are a few
who believe her death
the best death you can have.

Spit

I've been spit at, marching for a cause,
shouts, "We know who you are" from the mob,
but I haven't done or said anything for years
worth being spit at.
I keep away from places where
if I just stood, looking as I do,
I could find spit and my killer.
I've been spit at by snakes,
grasshoppers and alpacas.
I know spit stories.
Jesus spit on mud and cured a blind man.
I heard a Welsh poet say to a Scots poet,
"I'd spit in your eye,
but there's so much spit there already
it wouldn't fit." Enough. Out of their spit
Egyptian gods made children,
while Saturn ate and spit out his sons,
we needed Eden and a virgin birth. Naked
Eve ate the mouthwatering fruit of knowledge—
mortality came with spit.

*

Spit is sometimes sad,
omnipresent, it is kept out of mind—
there's so much poetry of the senses,
does spit want to be a tear?
Spit was not made to lick postage stamps,
but without spit we die screaming
from a cracked mouth full of death.
It shows family history, has quality.
No doubt, you can get a good price
for a flask or handkerchief of royal slaver—

the proceeds given to charity.
Yes, spit anywhere can be sexual—
everything depends on the mouth.
If you can't take a little dog spit,
stay out of my house.

*

I did not spit in the face of John Donne.
When the yellow wind is blowing,   .
a Chinese poet would value Godly spit,
its rhymes and half-rhymes.
We don't have calligraphy,
but we have spitting images,
a likeness in a cradle, a little face
of a grandmother long dead.
Spit was not made for a spittoon,
but it likes to mingle in a crowd.
Spit doesn't have a song:
spit is like the morning dew,
it would be happy in a brook.
All water is made by God who took
ocean, mud and bones,
made Muslim, Christian, and Jew.
    Now spit has a tune.
I want to spit to the sun and moon,
above the clouds, higher than hawks fly.
Sun and moon take spit as a compliment,
a new star. They have seen everything,
fires that gossip and sing,
how Gods can reproduce Goddesses—
Venus born out of the thigh of Zeus,
but no one has ever tried to spit so high.

Waltz

"Whoever shall say thou fool shall be in danger of hellfire."
–Matthew 5:22

Thou fool! Three score and six years ago,
I woke after a fool's daydream—
I received a pictureless postcard special delivery
from a former girlfriend in Woman's Hospital
telling me she brought forth a daughter,
her name and weight—I suppose, pride of her husband
of 7 months, a good doctor. I saved the postcard
during years of Reconstruction, pinned to the wall—
my bedroom was full of daughters without fathers.
Sixty years later, on the internet, a blessed event:
I saw a photo of the worthy doctor husband
dancing happily with his daughter,
the picture of my mother.
I saw online she was a piano tuner,
a profession of gifted souls.
Clearly she had love for her happy step-father.
She's childless, I do not know with whom she sleeps,
lover, husband, wife, dog, or cat,
or just *Eine Kleine Nachtmusik.*
She knows middle C from a hole in the ground,
no reason for her to know the mysterious ocean.
My father used to ask me who was I to think,
but I think she has a meantone temperament. Bless her,
she knows Pythagorean tuning, preludes and fugues
written in all 24 major and minor keys.
May she avoid the unpleasant wolf interval.

The child, mother to the man, taught me
fifths, fourths, thirds, both major and minor,
often in an ascending or descending pattern,
the beat, frequencies between notes,
then, of course, the psychoacoustic affect.
My overused ears tend to perceive
the higher notes as flat, compared to those at midrange.
I bought myself a tuning fork for Father's Day.

I think I'll go swimming, look under water
for a fathered and un-fathered daughter.
At 65, would it be better for her to know
which father is her father?
Could I explain the look on her mother's face
when her mother sometimes looked
for the Jew and poet in her Christian daughter?
Would my daughter play on her baby grand
the Great Deception Waltz
if out of terrible curiosity I told her the truth?

Review

A clothesline
tied from a dead ash to a weeping willow,
my old and new clothes washed clean,
on close look not washed, something to fool the eye,
my stained underwear and holy socks,
blooms of good and evil, and something to fool the ear,
dirty laundry flapping in the wind in meter.
I know bird chatterings are love calls.
Why don't they teach the "are"s anymore,
you are, we are, what are we to do?
Clothespinned to the line, my dirty laundry
often tells the truth, not the whole truth,
not nothing but the truth, so help me God.
Laundry makes nothing happen: it survives
in the valley of never-fooled sun and winds
where nothing is said by happenstance.
I babble, trying to honor the language:
"I am the world, a globe walking with long legs,
cities, oceans, smoking dumps around my waist."
When the music changes, the fiber optic lines tremble.
I hum the rest, I remember poets who made it new,
swam in the Yangtze, Passaic, Thames and Charles.
Like Hart Crane I wore a bathing suit with a top.
I thought describing the fat lady in the circus,
legs spread apart from the ankles up,
was the naked truth. Why are there no laughing willows?
There are giggling brooks. I heard laughter in the forest,
seven foot golden bantam corn growing in August.
It sounds like happiness, till 8PM above the Hudson,
when laundry, clean and dirty, is taken in,
when the night creatures I love come out.

Silence

Trees and flowers elbow their neighbors
out of sunlight and rain.
Born misdirected, to better myself,
I made an "In God We Trust" soup
out of vegetable pickings, not killings,
against the recipe: devour one another
to stay alive. In another universe
God may have corrected His mistakes.
I give Him, Her, Them the benefit of doubts.
I would steal, if I had to, His gifts of fire,
air and water. I no longer take for granted
the spectacular inventions, birth and ignorance,
the failed experiment: death.

I could forget this palaver, blame it all on bang,
unbuttoned chance, personal pronouns.
How did we come to be us, the swarm, the packs,
snakes like years wrapped around each other?
Do all living things celebrate Good Fridays,
holy and unholy days and nights,
a certain thoughtfulness, like two nipples
for twins, eight for puppies and foxes?
Is love a good name for all this?
If not—anyword.

Now, for a long dead Australian I love,
Bertie Whiting, I will consider
the just-born kangaroo: life-size earthworm
with almost legs dropped to the ground, blind "joey,"

alone in the universe, makes its way up Mama's leg
into her sack to suck—later, it jumps out,
grazes on its own half an hour—
a touch of fear,
first joy of coming back after being alone.
(A newborn Einstein on the ground,
given $E=mc^2$, could not, on his own,
make his way to his mother's tit.)
After a consistent 235 days,
the joey leaves the pouch forever,
whispers in kangaroo, "Mama, I'll never forget you."

In the world's boat, everything that is or was
causes me to praise and curse.
Praise plus curse divided by two
equals silence, not prayer.

Elegy for Elia

Three years ago, dying, in pain,
you told me to my face—"Life everlasting
is to be loved at the moment of death."
To cheer up this gathering, I recall
a fight you had with your lover husband
who said in rage, "If you go to California
I won't water your plants."

Elia, you Turkish Greek Ladino beauty,
all your life you served Dionysus
in the theater and unholy places.
He had power to protect you.
Where was the God of the grape harvest,
the theater and ritual madness,
when the laborers kept sweeping your cancer
and rotten blood as if cleaning a gutter,
tangled hoses, tubes in all your woman holes
and subway tracks? You kept your smile
with all its colors, as if you were a bug
in a bottle of formaldehyde at the hospital or studio
that once smelled of oil paints, linseed oil,
turpentine, and the perfumes you and Sappho
used a touch of in certain places.

There is still hope of deathly justice,
perhaps, perhaps, perhaps
an angel will come with a harp and sing,
the harp itself beautiful as the Brooklyn Bridge,
and flower pots on New York City roofs
your lover painted. An unknown psalm
in Hebrew in parallel rhymes:
O Elia, my Elia
your life was reason for the Lord, Ancient of Days,
with his 42 names to give thanks and praise.

Lord or not Lord, Monsieur Descartes,

silence is a sound that establishes your heart.

You made noise for the Lord,

noise is sometimes right, sometimes wrong,

war songs and love songs—

peace comes with a governance of good and evil

independent of Paradise or Hell.

Who in New York or Istanbul will deny the possibility

that a wind God, purple eagle,

will come and carry you off,

lift your body out of an oak crate,

its American dirt, its amphora,

carry you to the ancient olive trees of Smyrna.

Male or female, he will do unto you what Gods do.

We all become dust and morning dew

blown away from here to there

out there—how far? Take any number

and add a mile of zeros.

We are not resurrected, we are misdirected.

We will stand on stage again,

the congregation in the pit.

The play is called *Nothing.*

Sooner or later you, all of us,

have a second death—we are warned

like Cordelia, "Nothing will come of nothing."

Wouldn't it be nice if in the end we married France?

O star of many wonders,

 "always, always, always, always."

I forgot to say, to death there is no consolation.

Gardens and Unpunctuated Poetry

Gardens do not need punctuation
between the lavender and peonies
baby's breath and violets
commas do not offer anything to morning glories
or devil's paintbrush or roses
the way the world is made
fragrant scarlet orchids and sweet peas
are not in apposition
the thought that gardens should have semicolons
or colons silly as street signs in a garden
Stop   No Left Turn   Dead End

Save hydrangeas from the parenthesis
the gardens of Grenada from upside down question marks
save anemones from the circumflex
the Dutch tulip from the umlaut
may Apollo protect a thousand palm trees
from a single exclamation mark
the amaryllis from the em dash
even now an Irish wart from a Roman nose

Palm trees and poems under the sky
do not need further clarification
certainly there are borders and caesuras
in poems gardens and door-yards
we see the mass slaughter of living things
there are stops worse than punctuation
some may choose to read an ancient garden
from right to left

or as a field that is plowed from the bottom of a page to the top
reading a garden or a poem depends on the reader's
need to praise or to live near flowers and certain words
he or she may want to linger a while
on a surprising verb or lily

I cheer for the first crocus pushing through the snow
proof to many God keeps his flowers and his word
I have seen fields of cornflowers and poppies
all the life they hold cut in two
by railroad tracks highways billboards oil fields
coal mines shopping centers and motels
things worse than punctuation
because the ocean was once where the garden and valley is
perhaps the reason the potato has a purple flower
the reason fish know the dances of India and Andalusia
why a gardener has written a poem about the word *the*
somehow left behind by the retreating tides

I have found gardeners on their knees
and farm workers laboring in the scorching sun
no less reverent than praying nuns
sometimes the world intrudes on gardening
poetry and punctuation
on a scorching August day a black field hand
from my neighbor's potato field
knocked on my air conditioned purple door
I found his distress frightening
why was he suffering like a wounded soldier

entering my life knocking on my door

when there was no war nearby

in terrible pain he said something like   got a beer

I gave him lemonade and a wet towel

little or no comfort

something like punctuation

Tears

Forty years ago, I wrote I would sooner disgust you than ask for
your compassion. My tears are barley water. I give you my tears to
wash your feet. My tears are lace on my father's face. My tears are
old rags that do not fit me. My tears are spit on my face, I know
spit is sexual. My tears mean no more to me than my grocery bill.
My tears are produce I stand in line for. Crying makes me a child,
female, shows I am a man speechless about love. I would sooner
hold a porcupine than defend tears. My dogs may pull it to pieces,
get a mouthful of quills . . . it's too lonely. I can't take care of it. I
begin to feel the wish to kill—the thing is dangerous. I don't know
what it eats. (A porcupine is the other animal that cries with tears.)
I cover my eyes with my hands. I have betrayed the impossible,
my porcupine—the thing's alive, smells of urine. I look for gills,
see ears, I feel the weight of thorns and flesh, Christ's crown. I
went into the woods that know me. The trees remembered my
mother. Wildflowers taught me reality, like them, is just what
is. The leaves set an example of representative democracy. The
wind taught me chants and common prayer. The sunflower taught
responsiveness, the dew punctuality. Oh my teachers, where did I
ever learn my vices? Walking with you in the woods I have learnt
lust. Your lips taught me to be lazy. Your eyes taught me greed.
Your touch to lie. You have burned my woods . . . cut down trees,
left me only with a snake, the penalty for all those who search for
paradise . . .

For Good Measure

He painted his faults,
what he could not see clearly,
he was the better for it.
He painted the unlikely,
the *un* of things:
unhappy, unforeseen
the uneventful everyday,
an abstract all or the everything, the fibs
"breath poor and speech unable"
the circle and straight lines
of what he called always
the abcs of never.
He dressed without thinking about the weather,
what colors go with, dandy or maudit.
In the lift, by mistake, he nudged his neighbor
he barely knew. His hand too high,
he waved as if from across the street.
He washed his brushes
in turpentine, the sink became
a gorge of sunrise and sunset.
Friends phoned,
he answered, "Pronto,"
"Dígame," "Oui,"
on a party line,
the Coney Island of telephones.
He was proud his callers heard from one word
his preferences, he was a rubble king.

Ninety years after he was given light,
an after-dinner drunk, one time or another—*Strega,*
Chartreuse, Anís de Chinchón, calvados, grappa—
he could not remember

when he did not hear the knocking at the gate,
sleepless on port
he played the porter in *Macbeth*.
He said with his loaded brushes, he painted error,
impossible arguments—although they were studies,
his paintings taught
the mountains and deserts of hatred:
the Himalayas Atlas Alps Pyrenees, lost souls,
the Gobi Sinai and Sahara, to love their neighbors—
green valleys were children.
He was a citizen of mythos,
a migrant from the cosmos,
not part of the retinue of chaos.
He could no longer draw a circle.

One Sunday morning,
faulted, almost blind,
he wrote a letter in large script
that went up and down hill:
" . . . my darling, I can still paint what I think,
blind eagles and dumb gossips,
differences between fault, sin, mistake,
the unlikely less likely,
a few remembered faces,
the anatomy of my melancholy,
dung and scat, the Dead Sea,
Chinese bridges that are also temples.
I paint changing seasons, what I don't have words for,
because no two things happen at once.
A few painters said it all,
almost all, others have their right to pleasures
every horse's ass has a right to.
Kisses for good measure."

A Walk

I saw the serpent in the garden
when I was two or three,
the bone of my head still hardening.
I walked with my father who held my hand
crossing Liberty Avenue,
talking over my head
he recited Shakespeare: tragical-comical
historical-pastoral-Samuel.
He was learning lines
he needed for an exam.
I remember my feelings, not the words.
Some forty years later, he thanked me
for the Shakespeare he remembered.
I said no, it was I who owed the debt,
kissed him without regret.

Last Meow

Fifty stories high,
a colossal white leopard in the wintry city
is the upper half of the Empire State Building,
thanks to twenty thousand lumen projectors,
not just a trick, but a cunning cat
with other endangered species.
I hear its cry above the city traffic.
Let the leopard take over Manhattan, meowing,
growling with hunger louder than a fire truck.
I bring rats and gallons of milk,
as I will every day, hoping it will stay.
Sometimes it holds me by the back of my neck,
carries me wherever it wants to go.
I call it Poetry. I call it my pussy cat,
my kitten I've been sleeping with all my life.
My big cat reads, respects the stone lions
in front of the 42nd Street Library.
In the main reading room it works, studies
which monuments the cats of Rome,
Paris, and Jerusalem make home—
the periphrastic reasons, causes, why.
Poetry slouches its way up Broadway
north toward the Himalayas.
It takes me through avalanch and blizzards,
the sunlight and lanterns
of the Analects, Gita, Koran, Bible.
We roll together, I discover its privates.
The gigantic cat has got me by the throat,
holds me down by a paw in the snow.
I never thought I would go like this.
I always felt death was supernatural. If I can,
I told Zhu Ming, my Christian-Buddhist cousin,
I'll come back as a butterfly in winter
so she'll know it's me.

My Good Old Shirt

Anything is the same old anything.
I've become part of the thingness
of all things I see: for example,
I am partly chair and table.
Moonless, the night seems almost as it was
last moonless night.
I let my shirt, my good old shirt,
lie quietly on my chair.
Not trained in any religion,
I've become the thingness I see.
Angered, I have no saint.
I don't want to be awakened by Christian bells
or called to prayer by first light,
when you can distinguish
a white from black thread.
The sound of a ram's horn
does not call me to synagogue.
I throw kisses at an elephant God
and a God of preservation.
Let me be awakened by a dream—
I'm on a ship, torn open in a fog,
a jolted passenger,
awake to the everyday.
I sing of the universal,
the thingness of all things I see.

9 Chocolates

It was a shock for me to realize
I have not seen the Atlantic Ocean
for two years, not seen the truth she represents,
the beautiful and terrible world,
not embraced her or been embraced,
tasted and smelled her, knocked off my feet,
not heard her many languages.
I address her only with baby talk,
her face more familiar than any face I know,
the face of every woman I've ever known,
the most protective and life-threatening.
When I saw her every morning first thing,
there was always a kiss,
the stroking of my face and body going one way
then the slap on the way back.

I've thought I'd be buried under a loved red oak
on a day like this in August
when trees are happy and beautiful as a tree can be
except perhaps some in snow,
but now I prefer you throw me overboard
into the city of God. The Atlantic nods and smiles.
She's heard so much of my nonsense through the years,
seems to remember everything I ever said or wrote.
The tide comes in. She forgets everything I ever said or wrote.

The faces on the city streets and seabirds
all look very familiar to me.
They've got my number.

Numerology is familiar to me as chocolate.
Because nine means life in Hebrew,
I eat nine chocolates a day
from a box with a painting of crawling Aristotle,
Phyllis riding his back.
Nothing but ocean around me horizon to horizon,
I'm heading east, bound for Dublin, Plymouth,
Barcelona, Venice, and Pireaus.
Sailing, I've been known to trust only the stars
and my own hopeless intuition,
not instruments, even in a storm.
Always lost, I am free, self-reliant.
The first sight of land, I think is Ireland, is Norway,
—Ibsen, not Yeats or Joyce today.
After a while, I'm off to China using charts
 (after all, the Chinese invented the compass).
On my tombstone, thrown overboard, I write,
"Here lies Stanley. He knew where north was.
Sooner or later, he believed the world would be
an Irish / Jewish / Chinese / African fish who reads.
Now it is easier to write than to read."

The Seagull

When I was a child, before I knew the word for love
or snowstorm, before I remember a tree,
I saw a pigeon in a blizzard, knocking
against the kitchen window, trying to get in.
My first clear memory of terror,
I kept secret, my intimations
I kept secret.

This winter I hung a gray and white stuffed
felt seagull from the ring of my window shade,
a reminder of good times by the sea,
Chekhov and impossible love.
It pleases me the gull
sometimes lifts a wing in the drafty room.
Once when looking at the gull I saw
through the window a living seagull glide
toward me then disappear—what a rush of life!
I remember its here-ness, while in the room
the senseless symbol, little more than a bedroom slipper
dangled on a string.

My childhood hangs like a gull
in the distant sky,
behind loneliness,
it watches some dark thing below.
I saw before an approaching storm
the seagull stays off the ocean.
On a trawler off Montauk
I am heading home full throttle,

cleaning my catch of striped bass,
seagulls dive, fighting, desperate for the guts—
their faces inches away from mine,
every face different, a sight I never saw before.
For a minute I am part of the flock—
something rises out of me,
struggles, surrounded by their cries.
I drift, glide off like my childhood
into the gunmetal sky.

Merry-Go-Round

Early Poems

Peace

The trade of war is over, there are no more battles,
but simple murder is still in.
The No God, Time, creeps his way,
universe after universe, like a great snapping turtle
opening its mouth, wagging its tongue
to look like a worm or leech
so deceived hungry fish, every living thing
swims in to feed. Quarks long for dark holes,
atoms butter up molecules, protons do unto neutrons
what they would have neutrons do unto them.
The trade of war has been over so long,
the meaning of war in the O.E.D. is now "nonsense."
In the Russian Efron Encyclopedia,
war, *voina*, means "dog shit";
in the Littré, *guerre* is "a verse form, obsolete";
in Germany, *Krieg* has become "a whipped-cream pastry";
Sea of Words, the Chinese dictionary,
has war, *zhan zheng*, as "making love in public,"
while war in Arabic and Hebrew, with the same
Semitic throat, *harb* and *milchamah*, is defined
as "anything our distant grandfathers ate
we no longer find tempting—like the eyes of sheep."
And lions eat grass.

Song of Alphabets

When I see Arabic headlines
like the wings of snakebirds,
Persian or Chinese notices
for the arrivals and departures of buses—
information beautiful as flights of starlings,
I cannot tell vowel from consonant,
the signs of the vulnerability of the flesh
from signs for laws and government.

The Hebrew writing on the wall
is all consonants, the vowel
the ache and joy of life
is known by heart. There are words
written in my blood I cannot read.
I can believe a cloud gave us the laws,
parted the Red Sea, gave us the flood,
the rainbow. A cloud teaches kindness,
be prepared for the worst wind, be light of spirit.
Perhaps I have seen His cloud,
an ordinary mongrel cloud
that assumes nothing, demonstrates nothing,
that comforts as a dog sleeping in the room,
a presence offering not salvation
but a little peace.

My hand has touched the ancient Mayan God
whose face is words: a limestone beasthead
of flora, serpent and numbers,
the sockets of a skull I thought were vowels.

Hurrah for English, hidden miracles,
the A and E of waking and sleeping,
the O of mouth.

Thank you, Sir, alone with your name,
for the erect L in love and open-legged V,
beautiful the Tree of Words in the forest
beside the Tree of Souls, lucky the bird
that held Alpha or Omega in his beak.

The Bathers

1.

In the great bronze tub of summer,
with the lions' heads cast on each side,
couples come and bathe together: each touches only
his or her lover, as he or she falls back
into the warm eucalyptus-scented waters.
It is a hot summer evening and the last
sunlight clings to the lighter and darker blues
of grapes and to the white and rose plate
on the bare marble table. Now the lovers
plunge, surface, drift—an intruding elder
would not know if there were six or two,
or be aware of the entering and withdrawing.
There is a sudden stillness of water,
the bathers whisper in the classical manner,
intimate distant things. They are forgetful
that the darkness called night is always present,
sunlight is the guest. It is the moment
of departure. They dress, by mistake exchange
some of their clothing, and linger
in the glaring night traffic of the old city.

2.

I hosed down the tub after five hundred years
of lovemaking, and my few summers.
I did not know the touch of naked bodies
would give to bronze a fragile gold patina,
or that women in love jump in their lovers' tubs.
God of tubs, take pity on solitary bathers
who scrub their flesh with rough stone
and have nothing to show for bathing
but cleanliness and disillusion.

Some believe the Gods come as swans,
showers of gold, themselves, or not at all.
I think they come as bathers: lovers,
whales fountaining, hippopotami
squatting in the mud.

For Margaret

My mother near her death
is white as a downy feather.
I used to think her death was as distant
as a tropical bird, a giant macaw, whatever that is—
a thing I have as little to do with
as the distant poor.
I find a single feather of her suffering,
I blow it gently as she blew
into my neck and ear.

A single downy feather is on the scales,
opposed by things of weight, not spirit.
I remember the smell of burning feathers.
I wish we could sit upon the grass
and talk about grandchildren
and great-grandchildren.
A worm directs us into the ground.
We look alike.

I sing a lullaby to her about her children
who are safe and their children.
I place a Venetian lace tablecloth
of the whitest linen on the grass.
The wind comes with its song
about things given that are taken away
and given again in another form.

Why are the poor cawing, hooting,
screaming in the woods?

I wish death were a whippoorwill
the first bird I could name.
Why is everything so heavy?
I did not think
she was still helping me to carry
the weight of my life.
Now the world's poor are before me.
How can I lift them one by one in my arms?

The Blanket

The man who never prays
accepts that the wheat field in summer
kneels in prayer when the wind blows across it,
that the wordless rain and snow
protect the world from blasphemy.
His wife covers him with a blanket
on a cold night—it is, perhaps, a prayer?
The man who never prays says kindness and prayer
are close, but not as close as sleep and death.
He does not observe the Days of Awe,
all days are equally holy to him.
In late September, he goes swimming
in the ocean, surrounded by divine intervention.

The Lost Brother

I knew that tree was my lost brother
when I heard he was cut down
at four thousand eight hundred sixty-two years;
I knew we had the same mother.
His death pained me. I made up a story.
I realized, when I saw his photograph,
he was an evergreen, a bristlecone like me
who had lived from an early age
with a certain amount of dieback,
at impossible locations, at elevations
over 10,000 feet in extreme weather.
His company: other conifers,
the rosy finch, the rock wren, the raven and clouds,
blue and silver insects that fed mostly off each other.
Some years bighorn sheep visited in summer—
he was entertained by red bats, black-tailed jackrabbits,
horned lizards, the creatures old and young he sheltered.
Beside him in the shade, pink mountain pennyroyal—
to his south, white angelica.
I am prepared to live as long as he did
(it would please our mother),
live with clouds and those I love
suffering with God.
Sooner or later, some bag of wind will cut me down.

Hermaphrodites in the Garden

1.

After the lesson of the serpent there is the lesson
of the slug and the snail—hermaphrodites,
they prosper on or under leaves, green or dead,
perhaps within the flower. See how slowly
on a windless day the clouds move over the garden
while the slug and the snail, little by little, pursue
their kind. Each pair with four sexes
knows to whom it belongs, as a horse knows
where each of its four feet is on a narrow path:
two straight below the eyes, two a length behind.
There is cause and reason for,
but in the garden, mostly life befalls.
Each male female lies with a male female,
folds and unfolds, enters and withdraws.
On some seventh day after a seventh day they rest,
too plural for narratives, or dreams, or parables,
after their season. One by one they simply die—
in no special order each sex leaves the other
without comfort or desire.

2.

I open my hands of shadow and shell that covered my face—
they offered little protection from shame or the world.
I return to the garden, time's mash of flowers,
stigmas and anthers in sunlight and fragrant rain.
Human, singular, the slug of my tongue
moves from crevice to crevice, while my ear,
distant cousin of a snail, follows the breathing

and pink trillium of a woman who is beautiful
as the garden is beautiful, beyond joy and sorrow,
where every part of every flower is joy and sorrow.
I, lost in beauty, cannot tell which is which,
the body's fragrant symmetry from its rhymes.
I am surrounded by your moist providence.
A red and purple sunrise blinds me.

Lenin, Gorky and I

1.

That winter when Lenin, Gorky and I
took the ferry from Naples to Capri,
nobody looked twice
at the three men having a lemon ice
in Russian wool suits hard as boards.
Behind us, a forgetful green sea,
and the Russian snows storming the winter palace.
We descended, three men a bit odd,
insisting on carrying our own suitcases
heavy with books: Marx, Hegel, Spinoza.
We took the funicular
up the cliffs of oleander and mimosa,
yet through the fumes of our cheap cigars
we observed how many travelers had come
to Capri with a beauty. Lenin to Gorky:
"In Moscow they'd kill on the streets for the girl
who showed me my room."
Within an hour of our arrival
we were sitting in the piazza drinking fizz,
longing for the girls strolling by:
a mother, a sister, a daughter.
You could smell an ageless lilac in their hair.
Lenin warned, raising our level from low to high,
"Love should be like drinking a glass of water . . .
You can tell how good a Bolshevik she is
by how clean she keeps her underwear."

2.

It was then I split with the Communist Party.
Gorky welcomed the arrival of an old flame
from Cracow. Lenin bought white linen trousers
but would not risk the Russian Revolution
for what he called "a little Italian marmalade."
It was I who became the ridiculous figure,
hung up in the piazza like a pot of geraniums,
not able to do without the touch, taste and smell
of women from those islands in the harbor of Naples.

For James Wright

Hell's asleep now.
On the sign above your bed
nothing by mouth, I read *abandon hope.*
You sleep with your fist clenched,
your tongue and throat swollen by cancer,
make the sound of a deaf child
trying to speak, the smell
from the tube in your belly
is medicinal peppermint.

You wake speechless.
On a yellow pad your last writing
has double letters—two Zs and Ys in "crazy,"
you put your hand on your heart
and throw it out to me.
A few pages earlier you wrote,
"I don't feel defeated."

In your room without weather,
your wife brings you more days,
sunlight and darkness, another summer,
another winter, then spring rain.
When Verdi came to his hotel in Milan
the city put straw on the street
below his window
so the sound of the carriages
wouldn't disturb him. If I could,
I'd bring you the love of America.

I kiss your hand and head, then I walk out on you,
past the fields of the sick and dying,
like a tourist in Monet's garden.

Anonymous Poet

to Jean Garrigue

Sometimes I would see her with her lovers
walking through the Village, the wind
strapped about her ankles.
Simply being, she fought
against the enemies of love and poetry
like Achilles in wrath.
Her tongue was not a lake,
but it lifted her lovers
with the gentle strength of a lake
that lifts a cove of waterlilies—
her blue eyes, the sky above them—
till night fell and the mysteries began.
My friend I love, poet I love,
if you are not reading or writing tonight
on your Underwood typewriter,
if no one is kissing you, death is real.

The Decadent Poets of Kyoto

Their poetry is remembered for a detailed calligraphy
hard to decipher, less factual than fireflies in the night:
the picture-letters, the characters, the stuff
their words were made from were part of the meaning.
A word like "summer" included a branch of plum blossoms,
writing about "summer in a city street"
carried the weight of the blossoming branch,
while "a walk on a summer afternoon"
carried the same beautiful purple shade.

They dealt with such matters distractedly,
as though "as though" were enough, as though
the little Japanese woman with the broom
returning to her husband's grave to keep it tidy
was less loving than the handsome woman in the café
off the lobby of the Imperial Hotel
who kissed the inside of her lover's wrist.
In their flower arrangements, especially distinct
were the lord flower and emissary roses—

public representations now shadows.
Their generals and admirals took musicians
with them to war, certain their codes
would not be deciphered, in an age when hats
and rings were signs of authority and style.
They thought their secrets were impenetrable,
they thought they had the power to speak and write
and not be understood, they could hide the facts
behind a gold-leaf screen of weather reports.

It was Buddha who had an ear for facts:
coins dropping into the ancient cedar box,
hands clapping, the sound of temple bells and drums.
Codes were broken, ships sank, men screamed
under the giant waves, and a small hat
remained afloat longer than a battleship.

A History of Color

1.

What is heaven but the history of color,
dyes washed out of laundry, cloth and cloud,
mystical rouge, lipstick, eyeshadows? Harlot nature,
explain the color of tongue, lips, nipples,
against Death, come-ons of labia, penis, the anus,
the concupiscent color wheels of insects and birds,
explain why Christian gold and blue tempt the kneeling,
why Muslim green is miraculous in the desert,
why the personification of the rainbow is Iris,
why Aphrodite, the mother of Eros, married
the god of fire, why *Adam* in Hebrew
comes out of the redness of earth . . .
The cosmos and impatiens I planted this June
may outlast me, these yellow, pink and blue annuals
do not sell indulgences, a rose ravishes a rose.
The silver and purple pollen that has blown on the roof
of my car concludes a sacred conversation.

Against Death washerwomen and philosophers
sought a fixative for colors to replace unstable substances
like saliva, urine and blood, the long process of boiling,
washing and rinsing. It is Death who works
with clean hands and a pure heart. Against him
Phoenician red-purple dyes taken from sea snails, the colors
fixed by exposing wool to air of the morning seas near Sidon,
or the sunlight and winds on the limestone cliffs of Crete—
all lost, which explains a limestone coastline
changed into mountains of pink-veined marble,

the discarded bodies of gods.
Of course Phoenician purple made for gods
and heroes cannot be produced nowadays.
Virgil thought purple was the color of the soul—
all lost. Anyone can see the arithmetic when purple
was pegged to the quantity and price of seashells.

Remember
the common gray and white seagull looked down
at the Roman Republic, at the brick red and terra-cotta
dominant after the pale yellow stone of the Greek world,
into the glare of the Empire's white marble.
The sapphire and onyx housefly that circled
the jeweled crowns of Byzantium buzzed prayers,
thinks what it thinks, survives. Under a Greek sky
the churches held Christ alive to supplicants,
a dove alighted on a hand torn by nails.
In holy light and darkness
the presence of Christ is cupped in gold.
Death holds, whether you believe Christ
is there before you or not, you will not see Him later—
sooner prick the night sky with a needle to find the moon.

2.

I fight Death with peppermints, a sweet to recall
the Dark Ages before the word *Orange* existed.
In illuminated manuscripts St. Jerome,
his robes *egg-red*, is seen translating in the desert,
a golden lion at his feet—
or he is tied to a column naked in a dream,
flagellated for reading satires and Pliny's

Natural History that describes
the colors used by Apelles, the Greek master,
a painting of grapes so true to life
birds would alight on them to feed.
Death, you tourist, you've seen it all and better before,
your taste: whipped saints sucking chastity's thumb,
while you eat your candy of diseased and undernourished infants.

On an afternoon when death seemed no more than a newspaper
in a language I could not read, I remember
looking down at Jerusalem from the Mount of Olives,
that my friend said: "Jerusalem is a harlot,
everyone who passes leaves a gift."
Do birds of prey sing madrigals?
Outside the walls of Jerusalem, the crusaders
dumped mounts of dead Muslims
and their green banners, the severed heads of Jews,
some still wrapped in prayer shawls,
while the Christian dead sprawled near the place of a skull
which is called in Hebrew *Golgotha.*
Among the living, blood and blood-soaked prayers,
on the land of God's broken promises—a flagged javelin
stuck into the Holy Sepulcher as into a wild boar.

Hauled back by the *Franks*, colors never seen in Europe,
wonders of Islam, taffetas, organdies, brocades, damasks.
Gold-threaded cloth that seemed made for the Queen of Heaven
was copied in Italy on certain paintings of Our Lady,
on her blue robes in gold in Arabic:
"There is no God but God, Muhammad is His Prophet"—
for whom but Death to read?

Wrapped in a looted prayer rug,
an idea seized by Aquinas: the separation of faith and reason.
Later nicked from the library of Baghdad:
the invention of paper brought from China
by pilgrims on a hajj, looted rhyme, lenses,
notes on removing cataracts.
Certain veils would be lifted from the eyes of Europe,
all only for Death to see.
Within sight of Giotto's white, green and pink marble bell tower
that sounded the promise of Paradise,
plants and insects were used for dyes made from oak gall,
bastard saffron, beetle, canary weed, cockroach,
the fixative was fermented piss from a young boy
or a man drunk on red wine, while the painters
mixed their pigments with egg yolks and albumen,
gold with lime, garlic, wax and casein
that dried hard as adamantine, buffed with a polished agate
or a wolf's tooth.

At the time of the Plague, while the dead
lay unattended in the streets of Europe,
the yellow flag hung out more often than washing,
someone cloistered wrote a text
on making red from cinnabar, saffron from crocus,
each page an illumined example.
At the Last Supper the disciples sat dead at table.
Still, by the late fifteenth century
color was seen as ornament,
almost parallel to the colors of rhetoric,
blue was moving away from its place describing
the vaults of heaven to the changing sky of everyday.

Does it matter to heaven if a sleeve is blue or red or black?
In Venice Titian found adding lead-white to azurite-blue
changed a blue sleeve to satin.

3.

I think the absence of color is like a life without love.
A master can draw every passion with a pencil, but light,
shadow and dark cannot reveal the lavender iris
between the opened thighs of a girl still almost a child,
or, before life was through with her, the red and purple
pomegranate at the center of her being.
Against Death on an English day Newton discovered
a single ray of white light refracted,
decomposed into a spectrum of colors,
and that he could reconstruct the totality,
mischievously reverse the process,
then produce white light again—which perhaps is why
last century, in a painting by Max Ernst,
the Holy Mother is spanking the baby Jesus.

Goethe found a like proof on a sunny summer day—
the birds, I suppose, as usual devouring insects
courting to the last moment of life.
While sitting by a crystal pool watching
soldiers fishing for trout, the poet was taken
by spectrums of color refracted from a ceramic shard
at the bottom of the pool, then from the tails of swimming trout
catching fire and disappearing,
until a rush of thirsty horses, tired and dirtied by war,
muddied the waters.

A heroic tenor sings to the exploding sun:
"Every war is a new dawning"—Fascist music.
Death would etch Saturn devouring his children on coins,
if someone would take his money.
Of course his IOU is good as gold.

Turner had sailors lash him to the mast
to see into a storm, then he painted slavers
throwing overboard the dead and dying,
sharks swimming through shades of red.
Later he painted the atheist *Avalanche,* then heaven
in truthful colors: *Rain, Steam, Speed.*
"Portraits of nothing and very like," they said, "tinted steam."
Turner kept most of his paintings to leave to England,
his *Burning of the Houses of Parliament.*

Against oblivion a still life of two red apples
stands for a beautiful woman. On her shoulder
the bruise of a painter's brush—she is no more
than a still life of peasant shoes.
"You will not keep apples or shoes or France," Death says.
A child chooses an object first for color,
then for form, in rooms with mother, father,
Death, and all the relatives of being.

4.
Now this coloratura moves offstage
to the present, which is a kind of intermission.
My friend Mark Rothko painted a last canvas,
gray and yellow, then took a kitchen knife, half cut off his wrists
bound and knotted behind his back

(a trick of the mind Seneca never mastered)
to throw off Eros, who rode his back and whipped him
even after he was dead, till Eros, the little Greek,
was covered with blood of the Song of Songs.
Now Rothko is a study of color, a purple chapel,
a still river where he looks for his mother and father.

Death, you tourist with too much luggage,
you can distinguish the living from your dead.
Can you tell Poseidon's trident from a cake fork,
the living from the living,
winter from summer, autumn from spring?
In a sunless world, even bats nurse their young,
hang upside down looking for heaven,
make love in a world where the lion, afraid of no beast,
runs in terror from a white chicken. Such are your winnings.
Death, I think you take your greatest pleasure
in watching us murdering in great numbers
in ways even you have not planned.
They say in paradise every third thought is of earth
and a woman with a child at her breast.

Then

In our graves we become
children again
then we are grandchildren
then great-grandchildren
and so on, name after name
till we are nameless
free as the birds to sing
songs without words
mating calls, warnings
simple trills, for no reason,
that call the day is glorious.

A Visit to the Devil's Museum in Kaunas

I put on my Mosaic horns, a pointed beard,
my goat-hoof feet—my nose, eyes, hair and ears
are just right—and walk the streets of the old ghetto.
In May under the giant lilac and blooming chestnut trees
I am the only dirty word in the Lithuanian language.
I taxi to the death camp and to the forest
where only the birds are gay, freight trains still screech,
scream and stop. I have origins here, not roots,
origins among the ashes of shoemakers
and scholars, below the roots of these Christmas trees,
and below the pits filled with charred splinters of bone
covered with fathoms of concrete. But I am the devil,
I know in the city someone wears the good gold watch
given to him by a mother to save her infant
thrown in a sewer. Someone still tells time by that watch,
I think it is the town clock.

Perhaps Lithuanian that has three words for soul
needs more words for murder—murder as bread:
"Please pass the murder and butter" gets you to:
"The wine you are drinking is my blood,
the murder you are eating is my body."
Who planted the lilac and chestnut trees?
Whose woods are these? I think I know.
I do my little devil dance,
my goat hooves click on the stone streets.
Das Lied von der Erde
ist Murder, Murder, Murder.

Ubuntu

I salute a word, I stand up and give it my chair,
because this one Zulu word, *ubuntu,*
holds what English takes seven to say:
"the essential dignity of every human being."
I give my hand to *ubuntu*—
the simple, everyday South African word
for the English mouthful.
I do not know the black Jerusalems of Africa,
or how to dance its sacred dances.
I cannot play Christ's two commandments on the drums:
"Love God" and "Love thy neighbor as thyself."
I do not believe the spirits of the dead
are closer to God than the living,
nor do I take to my heart
the Christ-like word *ubuntu*
that teaches reconciliation
of murderers, torturers, accomplices,
with victims still living.
Jefferson was wrong:
it is not blood but *ubuntu*
that is the manure of freedom.

Hotel Room Birthday Party, Florence

Mirror, mirror on the wall,
who's that old guy in my room?
In the red nightshirt on my bed
I'm a kabuki extra. If I please
I can marry all
to nothing, snow to maple trees,
leap for joy over my head,
play bride and bridegroom,
an old and young shadow on the wall.
I can play a decapitated head
laughing in its basket of flies.
There are no clocks in paradise,
a dog's tail keeps time instead.
(Today be foolish for my sake.)
Which comes last, sunset or sunrise?
Nightfall or daybreak?
The day is Puccini's,
the street is for madrigals,
the celebration in the cathedral:
a skull beside a loaf of bread,
but for my grandmother's sake
it's a portion of *torta della nonna* I take.
It is a double portion of everything I want.

A mirror is a stage: I'm all the comedies
of my father's house and one of the tragedies.
I draw my boyhood face
in blood and charcoal
I hold my masks in place—

all the worse for wear
with a little spit behind the ear,
and because this is my birthday
like a donkey in its stall
let fall what may.
To be alive is not everything
but it is a very good beginning.

INDEX OF TITLES

COMMENTS ON STANLEY MOSS'S WORK

"It is time to celebrate the singular beauty and power of Stanley Moss's poetry. He is a citizen of the world, both past and present, one who seems to have been everywhere and missed nothing. These are poems, out of the fullness of life, that impress me as being all at once deep, strange, loving, bountiful, and a joy to read. . . . The damp genius of mortality presides."

—**Stanley Kunitz**

"There are many great strengths in this book (*The Intelligence of Clouds*): a speaking voice assured in its rhythms, a language both exalted and plain, a mind that can think to the point of revelation within its elected figures or images. But such poems as 'The Debt' and 'For Margaret' are not to be described in terms of mere virtuosity. Their power comes of the fact that they are genuine—that they arise, as Yeats said poems must, 'from the poet's deep and honest quarrel with himself.'"

—**Richard Wilbur**

"Over the past decade Stanley Moss has tapped into a well of feeling and a wealth of metaphor and memory that have made him one of the most moving and eloquent American poets. His rueful yet celebratory poems on the illness and death of friends are remarkable examples of his late-life creative surge. They are poems to read and reread, poems to cherish as they cherish their subjects."

—**Morris Dickstein**

"Here is a mind operating in open air, unimpeded by fashion or forced thematic focus, profoundly catholic in perspective, at once accessible and erudite, inevitably compelling. All of which is to recommend Moss's ability to participate in and control thoroughly these poems while resisting the impulse to center himself in them. This differentiates his beautiful work from much contemporary breast-beating. Moss is an artist who embraces the possibilities of exultation, appreciation, reconciliation, of extreme tenderness. As such he lays down a commitment to a common, worldly morality toward which all beings gravitate."

—**G. E. Murray,** *American Book Review*

"These phrases pass through my mind: The sadness of biblical loss; the prophet in Gaza without his God; the melancholy of the modern finding its beauty in loss itself. I realize that Moss has struck upon the one theme that preoccupies us all and fills our days: we are adrift between two shores. We no longer have the assurance of a spirit world and we do not have the confidence in ourselves to go it alone. In this book, Moss captures the theme in poem after poem with poignancy and keeps me reading to the last page, and then to reread them all for their sweet melancholy which is their beauty and so much a pleasure to experience. It is a paradox that only a master of his art can command."

—DAVID IGNATOW

"To reassert a Rimbaldian *alchimie du verbe* is one thing, to deliver the promise of its 'hidden miracles' is another, but Moss knows where to search. His work ranges from Beijing to New York, ancient Greece to modern Italy, from the Jerusalem of the Arabs to the Jerusalem of the Jews. Each site has its rich, troubled langauge, resources for Moss, who finds America in a swarm of butterflies and God in a bath-tub. This is not to say anything goes; the poet's own baroque language is intricate and resolutely historical. When the 'hidden miracle' is unearthed, it emerges as a tentative credo: 'I believe poetry, / like kindness changes the world, a little.'"

—LAWRENCE NORFOLK, *Times Literary Supplement*

"Moss is oceanic: his poems rise, crest, crash, and rise again like waves. His voice echoes the boom of the Old Testament, the fluty trill of Greek mythology, and the gongs of Chinese rituals as he writes about love, nature, war, oppression, and the miracle of language. He addresses the God of the Jews, of the Christians, and of the Moslems with awe and familiarity, and chants to lesser gods of his own invention. . . . In every surprising poem, every song to life, beautiful life, Moss, by turns giddy and sorrowful, expresses a sacred sensuality and an earthy holiness."

—DONNA SEAMAN, *Booklist*

"As grand in his generosity as he is in his appetites . . . the larger-than-life persona Moss has created and sustained is good to have in your head, and at your side. God may or may not be his co-pilot, but Moss has a knack for lifting my spirits into 'the sweaty / life-loving, Book-loving air of happiness.'"

—ERIC MURPHY SELINGER, *Parnassus*

STANLEY MOSS was born in New York City in 1925. He was educated at Trinity College and Yale University. His books of poems include *The Wrong Angel, The Skull of Adam, The Intelligence of Clouds, Asleep in the Garden, A History of Color, Songs of Imperfection, Rejoicing, God Breaketh Not All Mens Hearts Alike,* and *No Tear is Commonplace.* He makes his living as a private art dealer, largely in Spanish and Italian old masters, and is the publisher and editor of Sheep Meadow Press, a nonprofit press devoted to poetry. He lives on a farm in Clinton Corners, New York.